UKULELE
FOR BEGINNERS

Tips and Tricks to Reading Music and Chords in 7 Days

ACADEMIC MUSIC STUDIO

© **Copyright 2020 by Academic Music Studio - All rights reserved.**

This document is geared towards providing exact and reliable information in regard to the topic and issue covered. The publication is sold with the idea that the publisher is not required to render accounting, officially permitted or otherwise qualified services. If advice is necessary, legal or professional, a practiced individual in the profession should be ordered.

From a Declaration of Principles which was accepted and approved equally by a Committee of the American Bar Association and a Committee of Publishers and Associations.

In no way is it legal to reproduce, duplicate, or transmit any part of this document in either electronic means or printed format. Recording of this publication is strictly prohibited, and any storage of this document is not allowed unless with written permission from the publisher. All rights reserved.

The information provided herein is stated to be truthful and consistent, in that any liability, in terms of inattention or otherwise, by any usage or abuse of any policies, processes, or directions contained within is the solitary and utter responsibility of the recipient reader. Under no circumstances will any legal responsibility or blame be held against the publisher for any reparation, damages, or monetary loss due to the information herein, either directly or indirectly.

Respective authors own all copyrights not held by the publisher.

The information herein is offered for informational purposes solely and is universal as so. The presentation of the information is without a contract or any type of guarantee or assurance.

The trademarks that are used are without any consent, and the publication of the trademark is without permission or backing by the trademark owner. All trademarks and brands within this book are for clarifying purposes only and are owned by the owners themselves, not affiliated with this document..

Table of Contents

Introduction 1

Chapter One: Modern History of the Ukulele 4
    Modern History 6
    Benefits of Playing the Ukulele 11
    Mental Benefits of Playing the Ukulele 12
    Physical Benefits of Playing the Ukulele 14
    Emotional Benefits of Playing the Ukulele 17
    Why You Should Learn Ukulele 19

Chapter Two: What You Should Know About Playing the Ukulele 25
    What Should a Beginner Know? 26
    Parts of the Ukulele 30
    How the Ukulele Spread Across the World 34

Chapter Three: Tips on Learning How to Play the Ukulele 39
    Comprehensive Guide on How to Play the Ukulele 40
    Sizes of a Ukulele 40
    Holding Your Ukulele 41
    Tuning the Ukulele 42
    Buying a Ukulele 43

Tune It.. 43

What You Should Keep in Mind When Playing the Ukulele..... 50

Chapter Four: Tips to Learning Ukulele Music and Chords in a Week 59

The Various Chords on a Ukulele and How They Affect Your Play 60

How to Read the Ukulele's Music Notation 76

Chapter Five: The Top Songs You Can Sing with the Ukulele 94

Top Chords every Beginner must Learn!................................ 98

Tips Before you Learn to Play a Song 100

Chapter Six: Gaining Experience after Seven Days 114

Tips on How to Gain More Experience 117

Spreading your Horizon 118

Take Courses... 118

Meet other Players 119

Teaching... 119

Your Ears are Gold 120

Learn from your Mistakes 120

The Ukulele Festival... 121

Practice Everyday 121

Dynamics 122

Conclusion: Ukulele- The Instrument of your Dreams.............. 125

References 128

Introduction

There can be no doubt that music is one of the things we have that brings us passion, happiness, and sometimes pure unadulterated joy. While music can be created through the movement of the mouth, it is often more refined when it is produced from a musical instrument. One of these musical instruments happens to be the ukulele.

The ukulele, all the way from Hawaii, is a musical instrument that draws both awe and mystery. Are you one of those who are looking to try out this musical instrument? What if we told you that you could learn all you need to know in 7 days? Yes, it is possible.

This book seeks to guide you on a journey of self-learning. As you read this book, the ukulele will surely come alive in every way. You will be able to learn how the chords can be played, the numerous songs that can be played, and more, including its very rich history.

Furthermore, we will be taking you beyond the first seven days as we seek to make sure that the demands of learning and maintaining this instrument stay with you for as long as possible.

Here are some of the things which you can expect to get from this book:

The very first thing will be the history of the instrument. You cannot fully play it and appreciate all that it stands for if you do not have an inkling of the journey it has been on and how it is currently known. Therefore, get ready for some of the best, juicy details explaining the history in its entirety.

Ever wondered what you have to do and know when learning about the ukulele? If you have ever wondered about that, this book will surely help you. Knowing the very basics is the first step toward ensuring that you make progress and play your ukulele in just a week.

We will also not drop you just like that after teaching you! This book will give you insight on how you can go about making sure that you keep gaining practical experience in your playing days.

Other things that you will learn are:

a) A fast way to read chords on the ukulele. Playing around with chords is one of the major things any aspiring musician needs to learn, and a lot of beginners struggle with this. If you can learn to play the chords on the ukulele, the potential of becoming a pro in a short amount of time becomes possible.

b) How to gain experience with the ukulele. After learning to play the ukulele and mastering all the techniques, what happens next? One beautiful thing about the ukulele is its worldwide use and prominence, so you will be a valuable asset anywhere you go. It is never enough to just learn what you need to learn. The world needs to be blessed by your gift, and there is world full of people you need to inspire. In this book, you will learn the top ways you can gain experience and attract a huge following because of your skill. You can be sure that as you read this book, you will never play the ukulele in the same way again. It will forever strengthen your love and change your vision of the instrument.

You will learn more about the ukulele and how it compares with its cousin instrument, the guitar. Ever wondered how you can effectively read musical notation on a piece of music and have it sound amazing when played on the ukulele? If you have, then this book will surely prove to be quite informative.

Are you ready to start this adventure? Turn the page and let the journey begin!

Chapter One

Modern History of the Ukulele

The ukulele is a Hawaiian string instrument which falls under the family of guitars. But unlike the guitar and other string instruments that are primarily made up of steel strings, the ukulele is made up of nylon strings. Developed in the 19th century, it was a modification of the Portuguese instrument known to be the machete. It is often described to be the hybrid of the figure-eight body shape of the machete and the string tuning of the rajão. It is commonly available in four sizes: concert, tenor, soprano, and baritone.

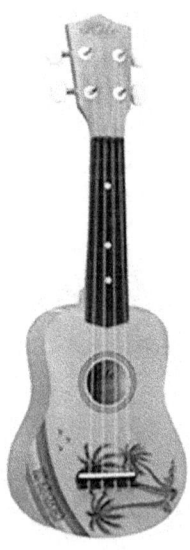

Introduced in Hawaii by Portuguese migrants, it was initially made from a wood known as acacia koa and composed of only four strings. Over the years, other materials other than wood, such as plastics, have been used to produce it. One reason why the figure-eight shape was not used strictly was because of its market appeal. This musical instrument enjoyed a major boom within the 20th century, which led to its spread worldwide due to the earnest efforts of some notable personalities.

In this chapter, our focus will be directed toward three major aspects concerned with the ukulele.

We will be examining the history of this beautiful instrument. We will also take a look at how the ukulele got into Hawaii and what led to the migration of the Portuguese in the first place. We will also consider why Hawaii was a destination for immigrants and the pioneers who started the development of the ukulele. We will also take a look at how it became a part of the Hawaiian culture. The royalties and dignitaries who promoted its use and how it got spread to other parts of the world will also be considered. It's sure to be a wonderful chapter.

The benefits that come with learning the ukulele is crucial for many reasons. Understanding these benefits will serve as a stimulant for you in your quest to become a ukulele player. These benefits are considered in three major categories - the mental, physical, and emotional benefits. These categories are not just outlined but discussed in detail, using a simple and easy to understand approach on what you stand to gain.

Finally, we will take a look at the reasons that should arouse you into playing the ukulele. These reasons, too, are discussed in full detail. They are quite different from the benefits you stand to gain. While considering this, we can come to understand why it takes such a short period, just seven days, to learn the ukulele sufficiently as a beginner.

After consideration of this chapter, your appreciation for this beautiful ukulele musical instrument will grow. You will be motivated to explore the other chapters that will serve as a practical guide in your musical development.

Modern History

The word, "ukulele," was in existence long before the instrument arrived on Hawaiian shores. It roughly translates to mean jumping flea, from two words; 'uke' with the 'okina, meaning flea and 'lele,' meaning to jump. The origin of this instrument is dated as far back as the late 1800s.

It all started when the first organized emigrants from Portugal to Hawaii in 1878. There were 120 members onboard from Madeira. Madeira is an island filled with music-loving people who were popular for the use of a musical instrument known as machete de Braga. The island of Madeira was known for its booming wine industry. But during the mid-1800s, the islanders faced a series of challenges like natural disasters, which led to great poverty afflicting its citizens. This necessitated the evacuation of scores of the unemployed populace in search of greener pastures outside the shores of Madeira. This was what led to the journey to Hawaii.

The Hawaiian Islands, on the other hand, was known to have a booming sugar industry. However, within the same period when those in Madeira faced a crisis, they also needed more laborers. Disease had affected their labor force, and they were in search of more manpower. So on August 23, 1879, 423 immigrants descended from the British ship Ravenscrag at Honolulu Harbor.

In excitement, after a four-month voyage and having finally arrived safely at the harbor, they launched into singing and dancing with the machete with Joao Fernandez taking the lead. Upon their arrival, the musicians who were all from Portugal were immediately quite popular. This was partly due to the many concerts which they held during that period. These concerts had a way of appealing to the people. They were true performers with the magic instruments in their hands. Sure enough, this event was not one which will be easily forgotten, and it found its way into the Hawaiian Gazette.

Among the immigrants were Manuel Nunes, Augusto Dias, and Jose does Espirito, whose professions were furniture and woodworking. After they had fulfilled their contractual obligations (3 years) by working in sugar plantations, they decided to settle in Honolulu, the capital, and a commercially thriving city, especially in the wood business.

These were the pioneers in the making of this instrument called the ukulele. The most successful among the three was Manuel Nunes, who was still in the business of making ukulele when it started to pave ways on the American mainland. His children continued on this same path of business.

They came up with a musical instrument called the ukulele, which was a modified version of the machete. This instrument is often described as a combination of the machete, which was shaped like a figure of eight and a five-stringed instrument which has the very essence of the rajão.

The pioneers or personalities who made it famous were King David Kalakaua, who was also a lover of the ukulele himself and earned the nickname, "The Merrie Monarch" due to his love for merriment. The king was very fond of the ukulele. He made it part of the Hawaiian culture. To reignite interest in the Hawaiian culture, which faced serious opposition from the missionaries who considered it uncivilized and discouraged the citizens from participating. However, the king sought ways to fuse modern art forms with traditional Hawaiian culture.

In recounting the kind of personality, the king possessed, Joao Fernandez, a renowned musician, discussed how the king lived in the Paradise of the Pacific Magazine, 1922. He also sang a song about the king's bungalow and how lots of people came. This song was meant to portray the personality of the king and portray it, it did.

The ukulele began to spread worldwide gradually, and the earliest commercial performance recorded on mainland America was at the 1893 World's Columbia Exhibition in Chicago and the Panama Exposition of the Panama-Pacific. This was held in 1915 in San Francisco. It created a lasting impression on the minds of those in attendance. This exposition was in celebration of the Panama Canal, which linked both the Atlantic and Pacific oceans. There were 24 countries present, and 17 million people attended. Four years prior to the commencement of this exposition, the Hawaiian Exposition Commission began to start organizing the exhibitions that led to its success in 1915.

These exhibitions were centered on the Hawaiian quintet, which sang melodious songs accompanied by the ukulele. And the exhibitions were appealing to lots of people who led so many to take on lessons to learn ukulele. A notable personality was Henry Ford, who was impressed with the exhibition and decided to hire the Hawaiian quintet to come over to Detroit at the end of the Panama Pacific International Exposition by December 1915. They were to perform for Ford Motor Company events all over the Midwest.

So within 1915-1920, the ukulele continued to grow in prominence. Soon, it led to tensions between the Hawaiian-base manufacturers and the American mainland musical instrument manufacturers and manufacturers in New York who wanted to capitalize on this opportunity to maximize profits. Regardless of this, it continued to grow in acceptance, which led to inexpensive models being produced in thousands throughout the 1920s.

As the years went by, the ukulele continued to grow in popularity. Notably, in the 1950s, some American servicemen that fought in the Second World War brought this instrument from Hawaii back to the US.

It also gained popularity in other parts of the world, like Japan and Canada. In 1929, Hawaiian-born Yukihiko Haida introduced the instrument upon his return to Japan. In 1959, he opened the Nihon Ukulele Association while in Canada, there existed a program that was aimed at fostering music literacy in the classrooms, making use of the ukulele as its primary instrument. Educator J. Chalmers Doane initiated it in the 1960s. It was subsequently revised. At about this time, the ukulele was also popular in the UK and played by Joe Brown.

In recent years especially from the 1990s to date, the ukulele has enjoyed a steady growth in its revival. Also, the advent of YouTube has aroused the interest of a lot of people wanting to learn the ukulele. We find practical lessons and tutorials online that come at little or no cost. We also find music superstars making renditions, using the ukulele to cover old legendary songs. A great example of such is Twenty-One Pilot's cover. This was released in 2012 by Elvis Presley. His song "Can't Help Falling in Love" was released in 1961. He sang this song using the ukulele as his sole musical instrument. That video on YouTube now has over 135 million views. The ease of strumming, along with popular songs, has appealed to many people. Due to its affordability combined with few chords and less time spent in getting a grasp of its basics, it appealed to people. Most people also identified it as a good instrument for beginners who have the desire to learn other string instruments. This is similar to other instruments. Hence, it is perfect for rookies.

Benefits of Playing the Ukulele

Often, we ponder over the benefits associated with a task before venturing into it. This usually serves as a source of motivation to carry on even in times of difficulty. For some, the idea of ever learning how to play an instrument seems to look like an insurmountable task especially when you consider a stringed instrument, thinking of how you can master the notes, keys, the pace at which such an instrument is played, rhythm, pitch, sound quality, etc., can make the desire you once had that shined so brightly grow dim. However, you can overcome such fear. This can be done by pondering over the numerous benefits you are sure to derive from playing the ukulele. Its benefits far outweigh any reasons for fear. Let's take a look at what you stand to gain.

We will be discussing these benefits in three major categories: Mental, Physical, and Emotional benefits.

Mental Benefits of Playing the Ukulele

1. It boosts your concentration skills. Taking into consideration that playing a stringed instrument requires a high level of concentration. It will be evident from the sound produced by any player if there is a lack of concentration, and it could end in pure disaster. So if you regularly play the ukulele, try to pay attention to every little detail. This will ensure that you have the edge and get ever closer to perfection. Perfection is the fastest route to becoming a professional ukulele player.

2. It helps to harness the great potential of the human brain. Scientists have helped us to see that much of our brain's ability is not made use of. Well, playing instruments such as the ukulele is a fine way of exercising the brain mentally and putting it into serious and healthy tasks. So this helps to keep the brain healthy. This also supported by research. A study shows that there is a lower chance of musicians having memory issues.

3. This is an awesome way to improve one's abilities in reading and comprehension. Musical notes, made up of signs and symbols, need to be understood properly before the actual music is played properly. Playing the ukulele poses us with the task of being able to comprehend these notes on seeing them. As we improve on this aspect, our daily reading and comprehension tasks will become easier to deal with.

4. Another mental benefit associated with playing the ukulele is that it can improve your mathematical skills. This comes as a result of our being required to count both notes and rhythms while reading music. Also, you are exposed to musical theories when playing music, and they contain many mathematical concepts. So having a grasp on them will invariably lead to our mathematical abilities being improved.

5. Playing the ukulele is a fine way to gain relief from mental stress. It is commonly said that music is life. Having a particular instrument you take delight in playing, like the ukulele, is a fine way to ease the stress after a hectic day.

6. It helps instill and improve your ability to be self-disciplined. To learn the ukulele requires one to be disciplined. You need discipline to practice over and over again just to be good at it. Without it, you could give up along the way. Increased self-discipline can affect other aspects of our lives positively as it even takes discipline to obey instructions that we receive from higher authorities, some of which we don't agree with. Increased self-control will enable us not to easily give up on other pursuits in life, knowing that if we don't, we might come out victorious.

7. Our sense of responsibility will be improved. Having an instrument that you love and cherish brings further responsibility to take very good care of it. The same too

applies to the ukulele. It needs to be cleaned and regularly maintained for it to be in good condition to produce quality sound.

So if, as a parent, you desire to develop your child's sense of responsibility, apart from getting him a pet, you could also get him an instrument like the ukulele if he is interested in playing music.

1. It enhances our ability to work as a team. Being able to work as a team is an essential quality that is needed in life to be successful. 'No man is an island' as an English poet, John Donne said. So learning the ukulele allows us to be part of a band or an orchestra, where we play a part in the synchronized beautiful melody being produced.

2. It is a safe form of entertainment. Some activities people partake in their leisure time today have left them addicted to them and have shaped them with undesirable characteristics. Playing the ukulele leaves much of the control of what you choose to be entertained with, within your powers. The kind of music you want to play and the time spent is yours to decide.

Physical Benefits of Playing the Ukulele

1. It enhances your hearing ability. The ear, which is an organ for hearing, picks up lots of sound or noises happening around us. We decide which of those sounds we want to listen to. This ability of our ears is further refined and fine-tuned to pick up and isolate fine sounds coming out from

our ukulele when we start playing. So it will come as no surprise if you can pick out specific sounds in a noisy environment when others find it difficult to do so.

2. It increases the rate at which our body members coordinate with one another. For good music to be produced with an instrument like the ukulele, it is required that the eyes need to send images of the notes being written down to the brain. The brain coordinates the rest of our body members like our hands and posture to react on time. So the more we play, the better our rate of coordination. This, in turn, can affect other aspects of our daily life, which require us to react quickly.

3. Playing the ukulele is a good form of exercise. Though not all parts of the body are required to play it, the hands, arm, and back muscles are being put to work in the course of playing it. This is a form of exercise for those parts of the body.

4. It also helps us to maintain or develop a good posture. A good posture is essential in playing many instruments. And playing the ukulele may help us learn how to sit up straight and even walk straight, thereby avoiding the negative effects associated with having a bad posture.

5. It could serve as a means of livelihood. In our quest to make ends meet, being good at playing the ukulele opens up a great opportunity to perform for others and get paid for it. This could assist us in tapping into a potential we never knew we had- becoming an artist. If it happens, you can

have an outstanding career. We could also take classes on them, teaching others how to play it, and in the end, get paid for it.

6. It adds fun to our daily routine activities. Most times, our lives seem to contain repetitive daily routine activities, just like a train taking the same route on a railway over and over again. This can be really boring. A fine way to get away from boredom is to learn an instrument. Are you looking for an instrument to take on? The ukulele is your best shot. With it being easy to learn its basics, it allows you to play lots of songs you derive pleasure in listening.

7. The ukulele does not leave you with any sort of pain on any part of your body. Unlike other stringed instruments, like the guitar, that are made up of steel strings, the ukulele is made up of nylon strings. So you are not required to develop calluses on the fingertips. You can freely play it without pain. It is friendly to the fingertips, and therefore can be enjoyed by both the male and female gender.

8. It boosts our ability to comprehend and master other stringed instruments. There is a great similarity between the ukulele and other stringed instruments like the guitar and violin. Gaining mastery over this opens the door to explore other stringed instruments.

9. Learning the ukulele will not cut into your finances. It does not require a large budget to be able to learn how to play when compared to how much is spent on purchasing other

stringed instruments and learning how to play them. It is inexpensive to purchase and maintain.

10. It is not time-consuming to comprehend its basics. Due to it being an easy instrument that even a young child can master, it might not require you to devote all of your time to practice it. The time devoted to learning can be incorporated with other activities within your schedule. Unless you desire to pursue a full-time course in music and make it your career goal, then you can dedicate your whole time to it.

Emotional Benefits of Playing the Ukulele
1. It provides a therapeutic effect associated with an instrument. When playing this instrument, our mood brightens up, and this can help us deal with issues like depression, insomnia, and stress. The way we feel also affects the lives of those around us by uplifting their mood.

2. This is also another means to broaden our social network. When you play any instrument, you can easily observe that people feel drawn by the sweet music. Some of these people are professional instrumentalists or also have an idea about it. However, some might actually have no idea who you are. Most times, they can be strangers and other groups of people.

3. You get a strong feeling of accomplishment after gaining mastery over the ukulele. You feel accomplished. Finally, you've achieved another goal of yours. Thinking about the

time, effort, energy, and resources you have put into learning it can seriously boost your self-confidence and boy do you need it! The effect of an increased confidence level will definitely affect other aspects of our daily life.

4. This could also improve your personality. Since it broadens your networking society, you come in contact with various kinds of individuals with their unique attributes. So just like a piece of sponge soaked in water, unknown to us, we absorb some of their traits. This will affect our social skills and could positively improve our personality depending on the quality of persons we choose to associate with.

5. Reduce emotional stress. It is often said that music is a food to the soul, and we know the good effects a good meal can have on the human body and even our mood. Similarly, playing the ukulele can enable us to express our innermost emotions, brighten up our mood, and reduce our stress. So if you have been feeling a bit down recently, try to cheer yourself up with a little music. The ukulele is the perfect place to start.

6. The ukulele encourages self-expression. It is designed in such a way that you can express yourself in any language and culture you wish. The more you learn, the more you will be able to play any song you wish to play. Similarly, to a very good artist who can express his emotions onto a canvas to produce a unique work of art, you will be able to express yours, too, using your ukulele when it becomes a part of you.

After considering all these awesome benefits associated with playing the ukulele and other benefits you might think of, it is clear now that taking the step into playing it will be a worthwhile experience. So brace up yourself, be courageous and take that bold step into learning and playing the ukulele. Trust me; it will be one hell of an adventure.

Why You Should Learn Ukulele

There are countless reasons why you should get a ukulele very quickly and start learning right away. Here are just a few of them;

A Ukulele is inexpensive.

Compared with other musical instruments that may cost you up to $500 and above to acquire, the ukulele, on the other hand, just requires a range of between $50 and $300 to get a very good one depending on the size and type you intend to buy. So you don't have to worry about how you can save up before getting one or how deeply it will cut into your finances. They are not expensive. The ukulele is small in size and weight, which works in its favor as it requires only a small quantity of materials to construct.

It's one of the friendliest instruments for beginners.

The ukulele is made up of four strings, is lightweight, and has nylon strings. This combination makes it easier for beginners to grasp in less than a week easily. It does not require you to use several weeks to develop calluses on your fingers before you can play without too much stress. Its nylon strings can also be easily pressed down with little effort when compared to other stringed instruments. So even elderly people and young children can easily handle it.

It's easy to carry.

When you love an instrument, and it becomes a part of you, there is an urge always to have it by your side. But this is usually not possible for your guitars, pianos and most instruments. Mostly because of their size. The ukulele, on the other hand, is light and can easily be carried without too much trouble.

The size, too, is not as large when compared to the others. So even if you are making use of public transport, you will not cause any inconvenience for either yourself or your fellow passengers. Its size and weight also make it easier for it is handled properly by kids and those advanced in age. So they can enjoy a firm grip while playing as if it was an extension of a part of their body. Perfect, isn't it?

It's durable and not expensive to maintain.

Still considering the size here, you can see that the small size makes it sturdy. In other words, it will not break easily if it accidentally falls. However, you might need maintenance from time to time. A part that might require maintenance is the nylon strings. At times they might break due to usage or might get worn out due to age. Whichever is the case, changing the strings is less expensive too.

The ukulele can be used to strum most songs.

Being made up of four strings, most songs we enjoy can be simplified and easily played with the ukulele. Unlike the piano and guitar that comprise of huge ranges of notes and thereby making it difficult to play, the ukulele can be used to play such note and chords that have been paired to a simplified format. This feature enables thousands of persons to play along with the song they enjoy listening to regularly.

It's a great instrument for songwriting.

With its simple form, an artist could write a song and perform it on the same day. It does not require much work to be done on the sound and other adjustments that could consume one's time. It's simple form also enables an artist to easily express himself in any form he wants his song to be in, without necessarily being worried if he is singing in line with the instrument.

However, music has kept growing with the introduction of technology. With complicated musical technologies available today, an artist faces the task of trying to sing in a way that synchronizes with the sound produced. To do otherwise will probably mean the song won't come out well. However, with the ukulele, things are different. The ukulele eases all this and leaves room for you to be versatile.

Playing the ukulele is really fun.

While trying to learn other instruments, it might require that you take time to memorize the chords, keys, or note. This has to been done for some time while one learns how the instrument works. However, with the ukulele, you get a fun instrument. With it being easy to learn within seven days, you are bound to enjoy playing it even right from when you pick it up to start playing. And catching fun in doing whatever we are doing, makes it easier to get better at it.

Playing the ukulele can lead to an easy transition to other stringed instruments.

Principles that are used in instruments similar to the ukulele are also applied when learning ukulele. Therefore, the effort used to learn ukulele will be minimal if you already know these steps. Learning ukulele will thus give you a head start should you want to expand to other musical instruments. It will be wise to start with the ukulele if you have the intention of delving into the others. These basics lay the foundation for you to grab a good understanding of the others.

You might still be wondering why it's being said that you can learn how to play the ukulele in a short period of time. The next reason outlines why that is possible.

Ukulele's are easy to play and the patterns are easy to memorize.

The chord shapes are pretty much easy to memorize when compared with other string instruments. This is because since the ukulele has just four strings, it has been simplified to the point that you will require few of your fingers being used to play it, unlike the others. Take, for example, to play the C major chord shape requires just one finger. While playing on the guitar, three fingers are required to play this same chord shape. You will also find out that this C major shape is used to play lots of songs.

So with few fingers involved in playing these chord shapes, it's quite easy to learn the steps needed, unlike when more fingers are involved. When you have to use more fingers, you battle for a long time before you can get a hold of them in your memory.

In this case, you can start playing your first song in less than five minutes! With three simple movable chord shapes, you learn more about the ukulele. In turn, you will be exposed to thirty-three different chords. When all these chords are at your fingertips, millions of songs can be played.

The ukulele contains twelve keys you can play with. Although, as a beginner, the C key might be your first step. You should also learn the remaining 11 keys progressively. What this means you can have some good time right from the start down to the end.

Therefore, after a thorough consideration of these reasons, you will agree that playing the ukulele is an experience you definitely will not like to miss out on. Also, these are not just the only reasons that could motivate you into playing the ukulele. With your own unique situation, you can think of more. It's not too late for you to give it a try. No matter the age or generation you belong to, the ukulele is open to you.

Conclusion

Loving ukulele yet? Things can only get better from here on. In the following chapters, we will learn about the chords and how to read music. Other things, too, will be discussed in previous chapters.

These will include how the ukulele compares with the guitar and the various ways in which you can gain practical experience. This will be needed after the seven days are up. Learning to play the ukulele is a gradual process, and you are about to find out. However, at the end of the day, you should be able to play the ukulele perfectly. Let's ride on.

Chapter Two

What You Should Know About Playing the Ukulele

There is hardly anyone who has listened to the sound of the ukulele and hasn't been drawn to it. All over the world, more and more people are becoming aware of this instrument and have come to appreciate it for everything it stands for, especially its uniqueness.

Now, it is one thing to like an instrument, it is another thing to want to learn it, and for most people, that is the dreadful part. Most times, people simply want to put on their headphones and listen to the sound of an instrument playing and mutter to themselves,

"Oh, this girl/guy is very good. I wish I can play just like they do."

And this series of excuses keep pouring it, year in, year out, till their jaws slack, their legs become feeble, and their eyes become dim.

You certainly do not want to be like that and live an old-age full of regrets. That is why you are making the bold step to read this book, and you should be proud of yourself for that. Before delving into the mechanisms of the ukulele, you must know some basic things so that you are not caught unawares when you encounter them. Plus, you will also get to know how the ukulele became popular.

Shall we?

What Should a Beginner Know?

There are some basic things that a beginner should know:

Price Should Not Be the Sole Factor When Buying a Ukulele

You must get a decent ukulele, especially as a beginner. While most ukuleles come in different price ranges so that cost shouldn't be a problem to you, do not allow the price of a ukulele deceive you into purchasing one that won't last for a while. It is better to save up money to buy a decent, cost-friendly, and strong ukulele than to hurriedly buy either because every other person is getting one or you lack the patience. The problem with most cheap ukuleles is that they easily go out of tune. You really want to get rid of all those distractions by getting a good ukulele.

Learn the Basics First

The internet has made it look like most musicians, artists, or composers moved their way to the top without putting in the effort, so a lot of youths are trying to break in into the music industry without learning the basics. Do not be deceived by the easy way kids do amazing things on the ukulele. It is must have taken years of consistent practice to have reached that point. Learn your basic chords before proceeding to play for top people in the industry.

Once you have mastered the basics, you can successfully write songs with ease.

Take Note of Your Position/Posture

The posture of a person determines a lot of things, including how he/she behaves at that particular moment. Here is a very effective way of doing these things. Imagine yourself sitting or lying down and take note of the surroundings. If you imagine yourself sitting, the body of the ukulele should rest on one of the legs and then use the other arm to strum the instrument.

If you are standing, you can rest it against your chest and strum with the other hand. You are free to use a strap if you want, but it is quite unnecessary because it adds a lot of baggage to the instrument.

Do Not Expect Quality Performance at the Beginning

Always remember those good things do not come in a hurry. Do not expect the results that one person has with the results that another has without comparing the time they started learning and the consistent efforts they both put in. As a beginner, your primary aim is to learn the basics so that you will be able to play the songs you love, so do not compare your growth rate with a person who already has thousands of people following him or her.

The first thing you have to do is to give yourself a time frame, and specific days or times that you are going to work on your craft and be committed. The time for your craft to shine to the world draws closer every day you practice.

Know When it is Time to Say Goodbye

Some people may look at this heading and be like, "So a time will come when I will have to say goodbye to playing the ukulele?"

No - that is not what it implies.

Know when it is time to change your strings. Just like most fragile components of any instrument, they need constant servicing and maintenance. If your strings are out of tune or have overstayed its welcome, it is time to let it go.

So, when should you do this?

It is highly recommended that you change your strings after the first six months during the first year. Why is this important?

This way, you can ensure that the strings are still good for playing, and you will be able to train your ears. After this, your ear will be able to know when your sound is out of tune. You can then restring again.

Listen to Other Ukulele Players

No man is an island, right?

You must listen to another ukulele (most preferably, popular and world-renowned) singers so that you can draw strength and inspiration when trying to play your own songs. If you are already in a band, that is great. If you are not, you can join in grooming your skills. If you do not want to take that path, there are several free online videos. YouTube has a ton of resources for the Ukulele.

All you need is some inspiration on days when you do not feel motivated to play the instrument. Watch videos that will not only get you motivated, but will also help you to hasten your journey. You could learn a trick or two, you know?

Be a Guru at Recording Yourself

It is easy to get absorbed at the moment when you are playing the ukulele because it has a way of making us feel we are in control. Only when we record ourselves and actually play our songs back that we can point out our flaws. This will come in very handy, especially at this beginner stage, and when you want to compose music.

Two things are recording yourself does for you- not only are you able to spot flaws more quickly, but you get comfortable being in front of a mic, so it won't be a problem when you want to record for real. All you have to do is to get a comfortable position anywhere and make sure it is a place with no distractions or unwanted sounds that could interfere with the recording. Then start. You will be surprised at the outcome when you are done. The recording has a way of humbling people.

Have a Lot of Fun

After all is said and done, ensure you have fun when learning the ukulele. Do not be afraid to experiment and try out new things. Practice the basics and see how far you can go playing your favorite songs. You will have a following sooner than you expect.

It is also important to remember that concentration and determination are largely needed. There will be times where you will feel like giving up practice, or you will feel like you will never be able to learn the ukulele. The key is to never give up as a beginner. Starting the journey will always be hard and rough. The benefits of your efforts will, however, surely be seen at the end of the day.

The important thing is to have fun at every point in time.

Parts of the Ukulele

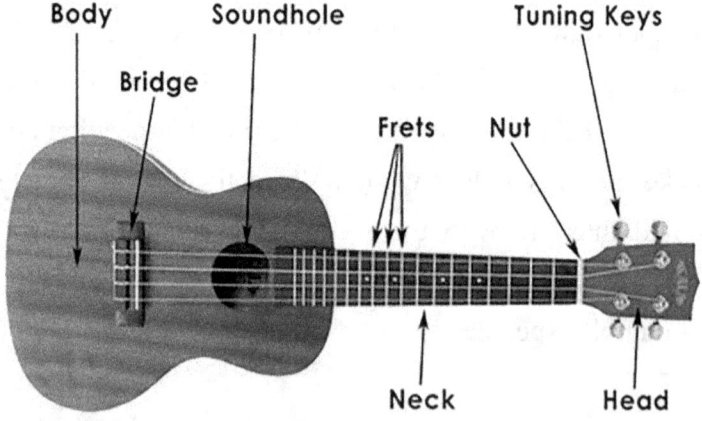

Several parts make up this amazing instrument. You must know the various parts so that you can appreciate how they work independently for a common goal. It will also help you explain the parts to other beginners when you need to impart the knowledge:

The Body

Relate the body of the ukulele to your normal body. Your body holds everything together, from your eyes, ears, mouths, legs, hands, etc. and each of these parts is located in specific positions. No one is greater than the other. They all have their unique responsibilities, but they work together towards the common goal of the body. All instruments have a body- piano, guitar, violin, saxophone, ukulele, etc. They simply help to position-specific parts appropriately. The body of the ukulele consists of a top, back, and sides. It is on the body that the designer determines the choice of wood that will be used. You must look for a ukulele with good wood so that it will produce full and warm sounds when used.

Bridge

No, this is not the conventional bridge that you are used to, but we will first relate it to the conventional bridge. You know that bridges are constructed to serve as a path for vehicles and people to move across, typically over large water bodies or busy roads. Without a bridge, many people will not be able to move from one end to the other, or they will find themselves moving around a circle that will have taken them less time to cross if a bridge was present. Now, no bridge is a loner. Some pillars support the bridge at specific locations. The bridge in the ukulele has this function. It is fixed at the top of the board to hold the strings in place. Simply think of the strings as a bridge and the bridge as a pillar.

Soundhole

Most people think that the sound hole is created just to make the design of the ukulele (or the guitar) attractive. They do not have any idea about what it is. Remember when we said that bridges are often constructed across large water bodies. The sound hole is carved on the top of the body, and the strings pass over them. They are simply used to emanate the created vibrations. If you have always been wondering what produces those fine vibrations, now you know.

Nut

This is simply used, alongside with the bridge, to hold the strings in position. While the bridge is at one end, the nut is at the other.

Headstock

The tuning pegs (which we will look at in a bit) are attached here and is located at the top part of the ukulele. This is also used to identify the company or brand that produced the instrument, and it has been very helpful in identifying various types. The brand's logo is usually on the headstock, and it may also have a serial number behind it.

Tuning Pegs

Imagine how people's lives will be if there were no tuning pegs. Like what will they do when their ukuleles are out of tune, and they have a concert the following day? Tuning pegs are lifesavers. They are used to hold the strings so that they can be twisted accordingly whenever there is a need to tune. If you hear someone talking about machine heads or tuning keys, they are simply referring to this. Do not be scared!

Fretboard

The fretboard is the black surface just beneath that holds the.... You guessed right.... the frets! It serves as a basis for the strings and frets. Most times, the fretboards are made from rosewood, but more superior ukuleles have fretboards made from ebony. Either way, it is one of the most important parts of the ukulele.

Frets

We have talked about fretboards, but what are frets? If you have a ukulele, take a look at the metal bars that cling to it. Note that they are different from the strings.

Fret Markers

As a beginner, fret markers can save you from a lot of errors when playing. They are usually little dots on the ukulele, but they can be more artistic and creative on very superior or custom-made ones. They are there to enable you quickly to know exactly where you are when playing. Take note of this order: they are fixed at the third, fifth, seventh, tenth, and twelfth fret.

Neck

Remember that the job of the neck is to support the neck and other parts of the body. The same applies to the neck of the ukulele. It acts in a dual capacity. It is a very strong piece of wood that acts as a link between the headstock and the body, and it upholds the fretboard. Sweet!

Strings

This is the ultimate part (no offense to other parts). All other parts work together to ensure that the strings produce very beautiful sounds. Strings are the things you pick to produce vibrations. Any instrument that has strings is called a stringed instrument. For instance, we have a cello, guitar, violin, ukulele, etc. Now, this is the sequence- when a player picks or strums the strings, the vibrations produced pass to the sound hole, which amplifies the sound to the body. Thus, the beautiful sounds you hear are created. As mentioned earlier, they are attached to the tuning pegs, so if your strings are out of tune, you know what to do!

Do you still have doubts about any part of the ukulele?

I doubt.

Let us proceed, shall we?

How the Ukulele Spread Across the World

From history, we all know that the ukulele has been around for over 120 years. How insane is that! Most of its contemporaries have probably faded into oblivion, with their history made known to only a few locals or none at all. But not the ukulele. It has transcended generations of civilizations, wars, and cultural changes to emerge where it is today.

Research has even shown that the number of sales of the ukulele increased from 2009 to 2012, and it doesn't seem to be slowing down anytime soon.

What is making the ukulele so special? Is it a unique sound? The Hawaiian heritage and roots? Or the distinct shape?

Let's find out.

It Gives Off a Very Friendly Vibe

The world is full of troubles. Most people go through each day, facing the hustles and bustles of everyday life. Parents are faced with the burden of trying to plan for their kids. School kids are stressed with both school and housework. Teens and young adults are trying to find their feet in life. There are enough reasons to wake up gloomy and sad.

That is why a lot of people cling to their friends or well-wishers that try to give off friendly energy, and this is what the ukulele tries to do. There is something about it that helps you smile and relax. The warm, tropical sound wears off the stresses of that day and brings you closer to your family and friends. Even if you want to play a sad song on the ukulele, it just will not fit.

Unlike other instruments that have harsh tones to them, the ukulele gives off as much friendly vibes as possible. Why will such an amazing instrument fade away?

It is Easy to Play

The importance of comfort in our lives cannot be underestimated. As mentioned earlier, most people run away from musical instruments because of the stress that accompanies the learning process. But most of the grandmasters have affirmed that the ukulele is not a difficult instrument to learn. In fact, in our age of easy internet access and the countless YouTube videos online, you can learn the ukulele without a teacher, as long as you have determination.

You can even learn to play the ukulele without learning to read music, although you will need to master basic ukulele music tabs. Can anyone say the same thing for the violin and guitar?

It Has a Beautiful History

Anyone that hears about the history of the ukulele is almost easily drawn to the instrument. Seeing it pass through several civilizations, going into oblivion for a while, and resurrecting with a bang in our modern times is truly inspiring. This is just to affirm the fact that good things do not die without a fight. In 1879, it was created by an immigrant to Hawaii, Joao Fernandez, and the name 'jumping flea' originated in this era. There was a huge rise in sales in 1920. However, due to the war, the music declined in 1930, with hard-die fans only playing it in their homes. In 1993, the ukulele came back to life with a medley of 'What a Wonderful World' and 'Somewhere over the rainbow' by Israel Kamakawio'ole. In the age of YouTube, around 2006, overnight stars were made with a simple viral ukulele video. From 2010 to present, the ukulele has been doing wonders.

It is One of the World's Most Comfortable Instruments

People treasure comfort and will not want to give themselves tasks that will ruin their moments of rest. Imagine if someone asks you to carry a piano or a guitar from one place to another, how will you feel? You will either be panting for breath by the time you arrived there, or back out of the journey entirely. But it does not apply to the ukulele. You can carry it and won't feel tired.

The Famous Songs that Sprung From It

One of the major reasons why the ukulele is popular today is because of the famous songs that were produced from it. We have "I am Yours," "Hey Soul Sister," "Over the Rainbow," and a host of others too numerous to mention.

Another reason why most people play ukulele is the fact that it allows them to connect with the one thing which they really appreciate. That thing is music. Music is what connects people in ways that we cannot even imagine. Having the ukulele by your side is one of the best ways to make sure that you take your love for music to the next level. Being a beginner surely does not last forever.

Take a sigh of relief, because you have done a good job. A really good job! Your consistent efforts will definitely pay off at the end.

We kicked off this chapter by stating some of the things a beginner should know before delving into learning the ukulele to avoid rude shocks. A beginner should get a good quality ukulele, and be mindful of his/her posture at all times, and first learn the basics. We also talked about the different parts of the ukulele, and they include the headstock, neck, tuning pegs, body, strings, bridge, fret, fretboard, fret markers, etc. We finally ended with how the ukulele became popular.

Ready to jump on the next board?

Let's go!.

Chapter Three

Tips on Learning How to Play the Ukulele

The ukulele is a fun way to learn a new instrument, and it has its amazing benefits attached to it as well. It doesn't matter if you've never played it before, learning how to play the ukulele can be quite interesting, fun, and easy. A lot of people view the ukulele as a guitar, but it is quite different from it as it has its own unique ways of playing. You could learn to play the ukulele in just seven days, as you well know. This book lets you know all you need to about the art of playing the ukulele.

The ukulele, which is pronounced as You-ka-lay-lee but is sometimes pronounced as a Uke, is a piece of an acoustic stringed instrument that has been compared to the guitar for a lot of reason. However, they are a lot smaller and possess fewer strings. It is considered as a national instrument of Hawaii and is made up of four strings.

There are several benefits associated with playing the ukulele and mostly because they are very portable due to their size and lightweight. If you have small hands or small fingers, no doubt, you will absolutely enjoy playing the ukulele.

It doesn't stop there as they are easy to learn, very much inexpensive and not difficult to find. Ukes are very easy to maintain, and all you need lesser accessories to play them, costing you a lot less. The ukulele is considered as a happy instrument and brings joy to a lot of people. They have been known to making people happier and more determined to learn the ukulele. This makes it all the more a fantastic option if you are looking to learning a new joyful, fun, and easier instrument. Although they may look like little guitars, playing one can be very different, so this book will guide you on all you need to know about playing the ukulele.

Comprehensive Guide on How to Play the Ukulele

There are various things you should consider before you begin playing the ukulele. A complete guide lets you know all there is about your journey to learning how to play. Playing the ukulele has been in the royal household of the Hawaiian people for a long time, and that is why it is considered to be a national instrument of Hawaii. Of course, for the royals to enjoy it, it must be what checking out, so other people thought, and gradually, the ukulele took over. But how to play and what to know?

First of all, a few things you should know include:

Sizes of a Ukulele

Did you know the ukulele comes in four main sizes, and they are all good in their different ways? The most commonly used or seen on is the standard ukulele, which is also the soprano. It has a body that is about 13 inches long and a complete 21 inches generally. The people of Hawaii designed this particular size, and since it is considered a national instrument of Hawaii, you will get to see this kind of thing a lot more often.

There are other sizes of the ukulele present, and they include the concert, baritone, and of course, the tenor. They all vary in inches, which is about 2 inches size up from one to another. The baritone is the largest form of a ukulele and could almost pass for a full-sized guitar. Some say it doesn't exactly sound like the other ukuleles anymore, but they are not guitars regardless.

Holding Your Ukulele

This is another important thing you want to know before you venture into the world of this magical acoustic instrument. Most ukuleles have a shape which looks just like that of a guitars although distinctively but since they are a lot smaller than a standard guitar, even if you can handle the guitar, you might need a little more practice on how to hold one properly to suit your comfort and prevent casualties such as dropping it or destroying it.

When you play the ukulele, you do not need to make use of a strap. All you have to do is hold it closely, so the back is held up against your body close to your chest or at the high of your waist. All you have to do is simply wrap your right arm around the uke to hold it to a balance. Have the neck resting just between your pointing finger and your left thumb. If you find the perfect balance for holding your ukulele, you won't have to worry about it slipping or dropping it. It also helps you play a lot better too. It is advisable to hunch over the instrument when you hold your uke.

The entire concept of holding the uke is to avoid touching it too much so as not to drown the sounds. If you can't hold the uke at first, don't go too hard on yourself as you will eventually get it with more practice.

Tuning the Ukulele

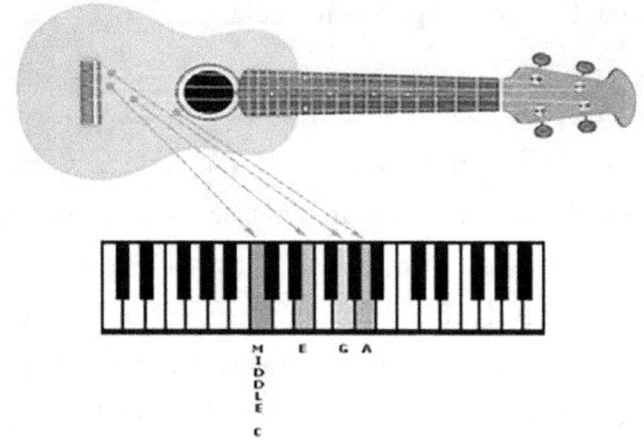

Depending on the kind of songs you would like to play, tuning your ukulele is very important. The C6 tuning is the most common tuning of a ukulele, and the order goes G/C/E/A. There are different ways you can tune your ukulele, and one of these is making use of an electronic tuner or making use of your piano as well.

The bottom line is, learning to play your ukulele is a lot simpler than playing the guitar, and it is such a happy instrument; thus, a lot more rewarding. There is a lot of guitarists who have played the ukulele as well, some including Elvis Presley, John Lennon, and Eric Clapton, amongst others.

When a beginner starts playing the ukulele, a lot of questions go through their minds just as it will when embarking on any new journey. If you're a beginner looking forward to playing this instrument, this comprehensive guide is here to help you through it. Here are a few things you need to do.

Buying a Ukulele

This is a very obvious fact. You can't practice playing the ukulele without actually having one. As mentioned above, there are different sizes of a ukulele, and the best to get started with is the most common size, which is the "soprano." Ukuleles come in great forms, but gear tuning pegs are more recommended for you than friction pegs. The difference is that gear tuning pegs stick out of the side while friction pegs come out of the back. This is because the gear tuning pegs are a lot better at holding the strings in tune than the latter.

Tune It

Now, as mentioned, getting your tune right is completely important because if you don't tune it, it gives off a not so great sound and deviates from the whole idea of making music.

There are various ways of tuning a ukulele, and the GCEA is one of the most common. Basically, this means the strings nearest to your nose are tuned to G, the one slightly above the middle is the C, and then the ones away from your nose are tuned to C, E, and A, respectively.

The strings on your Uke are numbered 4-3-2-1 from top to bottom. All you need to do is stroke each one from top to bottom with your thumb individually.

It is also important to note that the ukulele is tuned in accordance with the type of instrument which is in use. These instruments will include;

- The tenor which is about 26 inches
- The Soprano which is about 21 inches
- The Concert which is about 23 inches
- The Baritone is about 29 inches.

There are other forms of tuning your ukulele, and they include:

Electronic Tuning

The electronic tuner is definitely the easiest way to tune your ukulele, and it is pretty accurate as well. These timers can be found online and can also be seen at the local music shop. You don't have to worry about spending a fortune as they are not that expensive and makes everything a lot easier for you. When purchasing one, get the one that is designed for this purpose. You can also get a chromatic tuner, but the bottom line is that an electric tuner is a straightforward process, and all you have to do is place the tuner on your laps and clip it gently on the headstock before plucking the strings. This then tells you the notes you are playing, and you can make use of these pegs to get any note of your choice.

Standard Ukulele Tuning Method

The standard ukulele tuning is a common method, also known as relative tuning. It is called this because all four strings are tuned in relation to each other. This method is considered preferable if you are playing by yourself, and you want all strings to sound great together; however, this technique is not as accurate as of the electrical tuning. This form of tuning isn't the best if you are playing with other people. Here's how it goes.

1. The first thing is to use the 1st string, which is A, as a point of tuning other strings. This emphasizes how inaccurate this step can get, but as long as you are playing alone, you won't be caught up in many difficulties.

2. The next thing you should do is place your finger right behind the 5th fret on the second string (E string). You should note that when you pick the first string (also known as the A string), it should sound like. The second string can be adjusted with the aid of tuning pegs present on the headstock until you get a sound that suits you and sounds the same.

3. The very next thing you want to do is placing your finger just behind the 4th fret on the third string (the C string). It is an E note, and picking the second string should sound just the same. Another way of adjusting the third string is by tuning the pegs present on the headstock until you get a similar sound.

Other Ways of Tuning Your Ukulele

There are other ways to go about this tuning. Some ukuleles have a standard High G string, and that means all you need to do is have your finger right behind the 2nd fret on the G string and do that till a note is formed. As you pick your first string, it should sound the same, and the 4th string will need to be adjusted through tuning the pegs on the headstock to achieve similar sounds.

If you prefer a low G string, this example will be best for you. Place your finger right behind the fifth fret present in the G string to make a C note. As you pick the third string, it should be doing about the same. Fourth strings can also be adjusted with the use of tuning pegs.

You should have it in mind that this tuning process can take a lot of practice to master, but it isn't impossible. So you need to train yourself and practice a lot on your hearing and understanding; in other, it differentiates. However, it is considered a very quick way to tune your ukulele.

Piano Tuning

That's right, you can use a piano to tune your ukulele, and it is also an accurate way to go about the procedures. All you have to do is match the notes of your piano with that of your Uke, but it will take some practice as well.

If you have tried all of this and for some reason can't seem to get in tune, you might be using an older ukulele or a new one that hasn't be set up accurately, and this can make it hard or impossible to get your Uke to tune at all. This problem can be resolved as you need to tighten the screws of your machine properly. If that isn't the case, then it could be the strings that aren't correctly installed. You can change your ukulele strings with an adequate guide to show you how it's found properly.

Strumming Your Ukulele

Besides having to tune your ukulele, you need to know each and every part of this instrument. That includes reading all chord diagrams so you can change between shapes, and strumming is considered very important, if not the most important, part of achieving true ukulele sounds.

What to Know

There are various ways to learn how to strum your ukulele. You can begin with the basic hand position, and this involves a loose first. Then you strum with your index finger on the right hand while placing your fingernail side down. You should be hitting the strings with your nail when you strum. When strumming, it is advisable not to use your whole hand as it can get you tired in no time, so make sure to use your wrist instead, especially when using the fleshy tip of your finger.

To be good at your strumming, it is a best practice often, even if you want to try the advanced option.

Tips on Strumming

For your strumming hand positions, you should let your strumming handball into a loose gist and hold it in front of your chest (center). If you're left-handed, point towards your right boob, if you're right-handed, point towards your right boob. You can use your thumb to keep your strumming finger at a place for extra support.

Where to Strum

When strumming your Uke, going too close to the bridge can make the sounds a little tinier, and if that's what you are going for, then fine. The right place to strum on your soprano ukulele or even the concert ukes is right around the meeting point between the neck and the body. For those with a tenor ukulele, strumming closer to the bridge is a lot better for your ukulele songs.

What Are the Techniques for Strumming?

In other to achieve the perfect strumming pattern, you need to conserve your energy as you could get tired from irregular or too much hand movement. Ensure to use your wrist rather than making use of your complete arm. Your nails should always be hitting the strings when you are strumming down and when you strum upwards, your fleshy fingertip should be hitting the strings instead.

Swing/Shuffle Strums

This strumming pattern usually lasts twice as long as the average strike. It is very popular in jazz, blues and also Hawaiian songs. It is a very interesting strum pattern.

Simple Strumming Patterns

Better strumming patterns can be created by using the same up, down motion, and not hitting the strings on particular strums.

There are other ways to strumming your ukulele, which is very important to strum as it makes all the difference. When you begin playing your ukulele, you will probably make just the simple up-down, up-down, up-down gestures, but after some time, other things can be added, such as palm muting or slapping to achieve any groovy or funky feeling intended.

The ukulele is a pretty fun instrument, and even though you will love to learn it as soon as possible, don't miss out on the fun part. Some people could refer to the ukulele as a toy, but it is built to let you have fun while creating the perfect music, and that is a wonderful thing to roll with.

When you begin playing or learning the ukulele, never assume it is an easy instrument because, just like every other thing, you will practice a lot to master it, but it is quite easier to start and understand. As long as you know the basics and are willing to learn, playing the Uke should be a pretty easy ride for you.

Take It All In

When you begin playing your ukulele, you need to know about the basic strumming patterns basic chords as well, and with the time, you can start changing between chords. You can practice this with different chords and as frequently as possible. It is better to be accurate than be fast with your learning process and having it fairly decent. You can begin practicing your ukulele with fast and easy songs from YouTube or other places before gradually moving to more difficult songs.

You can practice finger exercising to give you a firmer grip on Uke and also record yourself while you play to know what you might be getting right or doing wrong.

To anyone learning how to play the Uke, it is usually a great idea to understand what kind of instrument it is and also train yourself on a background level. This either creates more eagerness to learn the Uke or makes you a better uke learner as well.

What You Should Keep in Mind When Playing the Ukulele

There are several things you should know before picking up a ukulele and deciding that this is what you want to play. Playing the ukulele might seem like a great thing to do because a lot of people are doing it and that's true, it really is a great thing to do and play with your free time, for your friends and family, etc. but if you want to do something, it is best to do it right. Here are some things you should know well before you decide to play the ukulele.

Be Committed

You should know that the ukulele is not a toy and shouldn't be treated like one. It might be a lot cheaper than many other musical instruments, but that doesn't diminish its worth. It might look a lot smaller in your hands and might sound different from another musical instrument, but that's the beauty of the ukulele, and it should be treated like that.

Before you decide to play the ukulele, you should be committed and understanding of its origin and how it came to be as popular as it did today. These may be theoretical, but it doesn't change the fact that it is a way to understand the instrument before proceeding to other things completely.

Success Could Come Later than We Expect— And That's Ok

There are a lot of articles only which swear that playing the ukulele is very easy and even tends to pass it easier than it actually is, but there is a lot more attached to it. It may not be as hard as another stringed instrument, but it requires time and practice.

The speed of your ukulele success solely depends on how fast you are at learning or how hardworking you are when it comes to chords and strumming patterns. So when you begin playing the ukulele, it is best to give it your all so you can succeed. With enough time and practice, the ukulele will be a smooth ride for you.

Don't Compare Your Progress with Anyone Else

Have you watched any ukulele videos on YouTube or Instagram lately? It seems all perfect, right? Well, it took hours and days and possible months of practice to be able to play like that, so as a beginner, or even as a ukulele player, never compare yourself with any other person but how you were yesterday. When you see a lot of kids on YouTube play the ukulele, it makes it seem like it is very easy, and you're just not bright, but that's not true.

Always have it in mind that everyone is not the same, and each person possesses their own strengths and weaknesses in various aspects. Comparing yourself to others makes you slow or makes you play for all the wrong reasons.

Invest in A Good Ukulele

You might want to know your budget before purchasing a ukulele, and although they are very cheap instruments compared to a lot, you will need to spend money to get them even though it's not too much.

As a beginner, the best ukulele is the soprano, and you can also get the rest if you want to know how that feels. Just make sure to invest in a good and decent ukulele, and don't buy yourself a toy as you won't achieve the same results. A good and standard ukulele will cost you about $100, and that's a pretty reasonable price in the market.

If you ever see ads claiming to sell you a uke for as low as $20, make sure not to purchase them as it will end as a total waste. It may seem cheap now, but they spoil faster, and you spend a lot more money on repairs. So why not buy a standard new ukulele for $100 instead.

Always Work on the Basics

Learning to play anything requires you to start from scratch, and the ukulele is definitely no exception. So when you start learning to play the Uke, don't begin with the hard part; instead, just learn the basic chords and learn how to tune your Uke. When you study them accordingly, you find playing music with the ukulele a lot easier and without as much stress as you will if you haven't. Knowing how to find your ukulele is also a very important factor.

When you start playing a uke that sounds out of place, it affects your music because your notes don't match, and it sounds entirely off from the music. This is why you need to check the tuning before attempting to play. There are various ways you can tune your uke, and some are very easy, such as electronic tuners.

Learn How to Hold your Ukulele

This might seem like such a basic thing, but it is actually the most fundamental thing to know when you start playing your ukulele. When you sit, you can rest the body of the ukulele on your legs and keep your strumming arm at the top of the Uke. When you stand, you can place and hold it against your chest while keeping it with your strumming hand.

It is important to know that your ukulele shouldn't be held to tight to let you feel the rhythm.

Fewer Strings are Harder

You might think playing fewer strings will mean everything will be a lot easier, but that isn't always the case. When you are dealing with a few strings, there are fever chord shapes to remember, and you can easily and comfortably switch between chords as you like. You should have it in mind that when the strings are limited, fitting different kinds of music because hard and even impossible for the Uke.

This is a reason why you will feel a little more uncomfortably switching to easy songs to complicated songs than the other way round, but with good practice, everything will turn out just fine.

There Is Hardly A Need for Speed

You might admire a lot of Uke players and see how much they play a song all too quickly, without mistakes too and you might think that you want to be in those shoes sooner than later and you just want to play like them, but there is more to playing the ukulele than play fast songs that a lot of people tend to miss out the details. Playing calmer makes people understand the song better, and all you have to do is to be gentler.

When it comes to playing with the Uke, doing it fast could mean little to nothing, so instead of focusing on speed, it's best to focus on the quality of the music as well as all the emotions you can bring out in people. Of course, you can always play fast, but it is usually difficult for a lot of listeners to catch up with the song, and everything just doesn't seem as right anymore.

When you have all these in mind, playing the ukulele tends to come a lot naturally, and the experience one you are sure not to regret.

The Ukulele Compared with the Guitar

The debate will keep on raging on and on as to which is better to learn- the ukulele or the guitar. Why this debate is intriguing is that the two instruments are very similar. Before we go deeper into the debate, it is important to realize that the ukulele and the guitar are pretty much equals. This means that while we are obviously team ukulele, we are in no way degrading the guitar.

That being said, here are some of the major talking points that are sure to pop up when the ukulele is compared to the guitar.

Price

If there is one thing that makes the ukulele better than the guitar, it sure will be the price. The ukulele comes out on top here. You are more likely to see the ukulele at a lower price than a guitar. For one thing as earlier discussed, the ukulele is smaller than the guitar and less fanciful.

Appearance

The appearance of the ukulele and the guitar is also one area where you can spot differences. For example, the ukulele comes with about four strings. When using the guitar, you are more likely to find six strings on it. This may vary depending on the type of guitar being used. Another difference will be the fretboard. The fretboard that comes with the ukulele is significantly smaller and thinner than the fretboard you can find with the guitar. It is also shorter.

The advantage with this is that people who have got smaller hands will find it more comfortable using the ukulele than the guitar. However, this does not mean playing; it will be stressful. While you are more likely to see other forms of the guitar, such as electric and acoustic guitars, the most ukulele will often maintain their original look (Hawaii look). However, you will and can get ukuleles that come with different colors and this embraces change.

The Sound

When it comes to sound, the guitar might be considered better for its variety. With the guitar at your disposal, you can have the acoustic, rock, or any sort of sound you desire. While the ukulele does not give you this choice, the sounds emanating from the ukulele can be considered to be unique. This sound is often referred to as perfect for friends who hang out on the beach regularly.

Even though the way a guitar is designed allows it to play all forms of songs, especially heavy songs, the metal genre is still open to the ukulele. However, experts find it easier to play such songs on the ukulele than rookies.

The Learning Process

For us, this is the most important point of them all. The learning process. Which of these instruments is easier to learn in the long run. That goes to the ukulele. You will find that you will be able to do so much more with the ukulele in such a short time.

One reason for this is the positioning of the strings and the tension it comes with. With the ukulele, the tension that can be found on the strings are much lower than the guitar. For most, the best option, if you are just a beginner, will remain the ukulele.

The guitar is more popular among people. However, the ukulele is the best musical instrument to start with. Hence, if you have made up your mind to use the ukulele, then you are surely on the right track.

Conclusion

The ukulele is a wonderful instrument for people of all ages. Not only is it easy to play, but it is also quite inexpensive as well. Another wonderful thing about the Uke is that you can take it, whatever you go, thanks to its portability. It offers you a fun time with your friends and family no matter the age you are, and that remains the beauty of the ukulele.

Children fall instantly in love with this little instrument, and even kids as young as five can easily play and hold the ukulele with much strain in their hands. That means they can carry it to class, to camp, etc. Basically, the ukulele is an ideal instrument for children who want to develop their mystic skills, so you might want to consider buying a ukulele for your kid next time you visit the store.

Even teenagers have embraced the ukulele and think playing it can make them seem a little cooler. It also serves as a new way to enter the world of music and learn a new musical instrument. The ukulele is a very friendly instrument you enjoy once you know how to play it and play it pretty well. It might not get enough of it. It soothes to mind and soul than spending all day playing games, surfing the net or watching television.

If you are an adult, you have nothing to worry about as you, too, can learn the ukulele. Lots of adults are getting into the life of playing a musical instrument, and what better one to play than the ukulele? It is friendly to all ages, even the elderly.

The ukulele produces a calming as well as beautiful music that can relax just about anybody. The great thing is, you are not alone and can even form your very own band..

Chapter Four

Tips to Learning Ukulele Music and Chords in a Week

Just as we have discussed in the previous chapter, we have seen that the ukulele is one of the most important musical instruments relevant to music in society. In the previous chapters, we have discussed extensively what it takes to learn and understand the complete workaround of the musical instrument. In the previous chapters, we discussed the various benefits of ukulele, which include the Health benefits and other general benefits, which are very useful, and the reason why you should learn ukulele is also given in the chapters above.

If you are at this point in the book, then I can say that you have done a very great job for yourself. By now, I assume that you now fully understand how important the ukulele instrument is to music and why it is important to learn and know about it. As music lovers and enthusiasts, it is one of the interests that you need to put into serious consideration. Based on its origination from Hawaii by Portuguese immigrants, the ukulele is very valuable when playing Hawaiian music.

A typical ukulele is shaped in the form of a guitar, and if you are not correctly informed, you may eventually think it is one. Most variations of the ukulele are often in other forms to distinguish itself from the original looking guitar, which people know of. In Hawaii, there are a lot of manufacturers who produce this instrument and also ensure that there is a proper use of this instrument. One of the major producers of the ukulele is the Kamaka, which was founded in the year 1916, and over these years, they have built a standard in the creator of fine and world-class ukuleles used by a lot of enthusiasts all over the world.

Okay. Enough has been said about the history and the use of the ukulele; in this chapter, we are going to discuss the various chords on the ukulele and how they affect your overall play. As a professional or amateur player, these are one of the things that you need to pay serious attention while trying to get deeper into the control and the creation of good music. In the later sections of this chapter, you will learn the various chord for you to know and for you to make your play better over time.

The Various Chords on a Ukulele and How They Affect Your Play

The main purpose of this chapter is to teach the readers the various tips and tricks on how to learn and play the ukulele in a week. You must take all the information given to you in this section seriously to learn and get used to this instrument. It is also important to note that you may not achieve mastery in one week as you start learning the ukulele. But, over time, with consistent practice, you will get to master all the chord outlined in the next sections and even more.

There are several crucial things that you stand to learn from chords. These things include:

The Technical Side of the Ukulele

By learning how to play the chords, you get to see the technical side of the ukulele and how it all works. You will also learn how many chords we have and the number of fingers you need to play each one. There is also the presence of barre chords. However, you can avoid this as a rookie. There's so much more to learn!

You'd learn the benefits of the chords

In life, you only come to appreciate something when you know the usefulness of it. The same applies to learn about the chords. The chords serve a fundamental purpose. They are the symbol of keys that are present in the ukulele. With these chords, you should be able to learn how to play songs. We shall discuss playing songs much later in this book.

Other things which you stand to learn about the ukulele is the interconnected nature of the chords and how this forms a foundation on which the ukulele is formed. It is simply amazing.

Before going further, we have to take out some time to learn more about the chord chart that the ukulele uses. Having absolutely no knowledge about this will make it incredibly harder to use the ukulele. Here are some things you have to know.

Meaning of the Chord Chart

Are you hearing the word chord chart for the first time? Well, a chord chart is a chart whose purpose is to show the five frets present in a ukulele. The chord charts will usually come with vertical lines. These vertical lines are often referred to as the strings. It also comes with some horizontal lines. These lines are often referred to as the frets. Together, they form what we refer to as the chord charts. Pretty easy, right?

Vertical Lines

The vertical lines, which are also referred to as the strings, have about four strings. These strings are often referred to as the "G," "C," "E," "A" strings. To play these chords well, you will need to make sure that your hands are placed at certain places. Also, it is preferable to play certain strings with particular fingers, such as the ring or index fingers.

Open Strings

Yes, some strings are present on the ukulele that is referred to as an open string. These strings are not meant to be played. There, make sure that your hands are never in contact with them. You have much better uses for your hands anyway!

In the ukulele, various chords take you to need to take note. These chords help you at any time, to know what to play. We will show you the various chords, and they can affect your play. The chord we will teach you about in the next sections is the important chords you should know as a beginner. These chords are the fundamentals, and in the steps to achieve mastery, these chords are to be taken into serious consideration. There are about 13 different chords which are present in the ukulele.

The most important chords are the C chord or C major, the F chord or the F major, and the G chord called the G major. To start with, we will first take a look at the C chord, which is the first chord you need to learn as a beginner. After this, we will take a look at the F chord and everything about it and the G chord.

C Chord or C Major

The C chord is one of the major chords when it comes to playing the ukulele. In the instrument, playing this C chord is often very easy, and it is very achievable. When it comes to playing the ukulele, the notes are simple and easy to learn. While you are learning the ukulele, the C chord is one of the first chords that you will need to learn. To play these notes, you have to use the third right finger, mostly. What you need to do is to ensure that you do not fret the G string, C string, and E string. What you need to know is that the G string, C strings, and E string are the top strings in your ukulele instrument, and by striking them at once, you have just let out the C Chord.

In this C chord, there are a lot of variations that can simply affect your entire play positively or negatively. While playing, you can choose to go high on the E note to improve your play. One thing you need to know is that using the E chord while you are playing makes the overall play easier and more interesting. As a beginner, you need to throw in this E note sometimes to add new flows to your play.

Dropping your index finger right on your 7th fret is also another way and another variation to play the c chord. When you drop your finger on the 7th fret of the C key, place your second and third finger in the 7th and 8th finger of the A string and the C string respective. By doing this, you will begin to see that your play will be a lot better. For the newbies who are trying to learn how to play the C chord but do not know what kind of song they should apply what they know, we will give you great options.

First, if you are trying to play a melody where the G note is the highest melody in the chord, you may use the c chord with the variation where you have to place your middle finger on the G string found on the 9th fret of the ukulele instrument. While your finger is on the G string, you need to place your index finger on the E-string 8th fret and the 10th fret of the A –string. This is now to place a melody.

Secondly, if you are playing the ukulele trying to learn a jazz song, you will want to try out a variation where you apply the index finger on the two strings at the bottom located at the 3rd fret. You need to place the middle finger on the C key located at the 4th fret, and finally, place your index finger on the G string located at the top G-string.

One of the biggest problems in learning how to play the ukulele is remembering the names of the note you are playing.

Finally, if you decide to play with a group of other ukulele players, you should also try out the variation where you place your finger on the G-string 5th feet on the C-string 7th fret and the A-string 5th fret. This will help you, especially when you are trying to make a lot of variations in your play while in your group.

With great practice, you can easily master the art of playing the ukulele within a short period. There are several positions you need to learn while you are playing the ukulele instrument. One trick that a lot of ukulele players do not know while they are playing on their instrument is that, when you are playing, you need to say the note you are playing out loud to aid memorization. By doing this, you will see that you will get the notes you are practicing faster and easier.

For the next important chord, we will take a close look at the F chord and how this chord affects our play.

F Chord or F Major

The F Chord is another important chord when it comes to playing the ukulele. For a lot of people, the F chord is a little more difficult than the conventional chord that we are used to playing. To play this chord effective, you have placed your fingers on several strings to fret.

How to play the F chord on the ukulele fretboard:

Before you play the F chord, you need to know that the F chord has only one flat key, and this flat key helps to lower the note pitch a half step. When we were talking about a C major scale, we know that it has no flat or sharp keys. This is the reason why we are learning the F chord because of only one note changes from a C chord.

To play the F Chord, you can use five different variations, and you need to refer to the C chord.

In this section, we are looking at five different positions to play the F chord and make good music out of it.

The first position is to place your index finger on the notes that fall into the 1st fret. You also need to put your middle finger on the notes that fall into the 2nd fret. You also need to place your 3rd and 4th finger on the 3rd and 4th fret, respectively. This position is very important, and it will help you learn how to play the F chord on the ukulele properly. To understand how to play this, you need to properly play the C chord, just like I have prepared in the previous section. To learn the F chord, you need to learn the C chord properly to excel.

The second position for the F chord on the ukulele is more difficult than the first position. In this position, you need to hover your four fingers in between the 2nd and the 5th frets. While you are playing along these strings, your fingers will also move to 3rd and 6th frets.

In the third position, you need to place your fingers on the two top strings on the 4th and 7th frets. While you are playing on these strings, your fingers are more likely to shift to the 5th and 8th fret to improve on the notes that you are playing.

Another way of playing this F chord is to place your first four fingers on all the notes that fall within the 7th and 10th frets in the ukulele.

For the next position, you still need to place your first four fingers on the 9th and 12th frets on the instrument. While you are playing on these keys and you get to the bottom two strings, your hands will shift to the 10th and 13th frets.

Just as we have seen in this section, the ukulele is a very simple instrument to play. Once you have learned how to play the C chord and the F chord, you will know that these keys are very easy to play. In the next section, we discuss the G chord, which is another important chord when it comes to playing the ukulele.

It is important to note that you need to understand what you are playing at most times. You need to be intentional in ensuring that you are playing with the right scale, depending on the music. Using the right scale ensures that your play is in sync with the kind of music involved. It is very important so that you will know what you are doing.

The G Chord

The G chord, or as it is fondly called, the G major, is also another important chord that you need to learn while you are playing the ukulele. If you have gotten to this point in this book, we will assume that you now have a firm knowledge of the C and the F chord that was introduced to you in the previous sections.

Before you proceed further in reading, you should know that learning the C chord is a very important step when it comes to mastery of the instrument. If you have not fully understood it, please go back to the previous sections and take a look at it again.

Here, we will talk about the G chords. The G chord on the ukulele is very easy to play. First, you need to place your index finger on the second fret. This second fret is mostly found on the third string. Also, place your middle finger on the second fret of the first string. In the G scale, the notes are G, A, B, C, D, E, F#, G, just like any other musical instrument.

You may play wondering. In what ways should you practice using the G chord? To achieve mastery, you need to constantly be practicing how to use these notes while you are playing.

There are a lot of positions you can use when you are trying to play the G chord on the ukulele. They are outlined as follows;

- For the first position, what you need to do is to place your index finger on the note found within the 1st fret. After this, you need to place your middle finger on the notes in between the 1st and the 2nd fret. Then place your ring and last finger to the 3rd fret and fourth fret, respectively. If you have succeeded in place this position, you will see that you can also apply the same technique on the C scale. The major difference between the two is that in the G chord, we are only raising the F note to the F#.

- The next position of playing the G chord is more difficult than the previous position. To play this, you need to place your fingers on the 4th and 7th frets on your ukulele instrument. Once you have done this, your fingers are expected to go to the 5th to the 8th fret.

- For the third position, your first four fingers should be on the 6th down to the 9th frets. And when you finally reach the bottom string and play the notes, your fingers should ideally shift to the 7th to the 10th fret. It will become easier to play when you dedicate a lot of time to play and practice these chords. You need to learn it all the time and make yourself better in the process.

- In the fourth position, you need to place all your four fingers, excluding the thumb on all the key from the 2nd to the 5th fret. This is one of the easiest positions to play, especially if you are playing with a group of other ukulele players.

In your journey to learn and master the overall play of the G chord on the ukulele, it is important to note that once you have a firm grasp of the C chord, a lot of things automatically become easier for you. It is also important to note that playing ukulele requires a lot of constant and consistent practice. In your spare time, try to practice with all these positions I have listed out for you in the previous sections. While practicing, you will get to know that there are a lot of patterns that repeat itself when it comes to the scaling and the way it is fingered.

A Major

A chord can be a major or a minor chord. We will be discussing the A major right now and the A minor just down below. It is important to learn the A major when you have fully comprehended how the C chord should be played.

To play the A major, you should be prepared to use two fingers. The two fingers that will probably have to be used will be the index and the middle fingers. Make sure that your index finger is placed on the C string. The C string will normally found on the first fret. As for the second finger, make sure that it is placed on the G string. You can find this on the second fret.

D Major

The D major takes the game to the next level. This is one major which will have to play with at least three fingers. These three fingers will have to be positioned in one area (2nd fret). Are you wondering how to play this? The first thing you will have to do is to make sure that one of your fingers is placed on the G string, another on the C string, and yet another E string.

It is important to note that you may feel a bit overwhelmed while playing the D major. This is because a lot of fingers are used to play one fret. This will be especially obvious if the ukulele instrument that you are using is a soprano or the concert form of the ukulele. The D major can be experimented with. While experimenting, the important thing is to make sure that C, E, and G strings are held down together. This opens up the A string in the process. What you do next is left to you.

B Major

If you thought that the B major was a bit challenging, then you should expect so much more from the B major. When dealing with the B major chord, you will notice that the chord being used is different. This is called the barre chord. The barre chord is a situation where one finger is used on at least two strings at once. Wondering how this is done? Let's try to finger it out.

To play the B major, the first thing to do will be to place your finger on the second fret. This is usually done with the index fingers. The strings that should be touched will be the A and E strings. Once this has been done, the next step will be to place your hands on the C strings. The C string will be located on the 3rd fret. The last finger should be placed on the G string. This string can be located on the 4th fret.

Are you looking for a good trick in playing the barre chord?

One trick will be to use the back or neck of the ukulele as a resting place for your thumb. This allows for more pressure through your thumb. It is important to remember or note that playing the barre chord might take some time to master. However, practicing some more should make the purpose achievable in a short period. Once you have learned the bare chord, learning other chords, and how they are played will become easier.

D7 Chord

This type of chord is usually called the 7th chord. Wondering what a 7th chord is? 7th chords are usually a combination of three chords. This can be accomplished with the addition of an extra note. The d7 chord is another chord where you will experience using a barre chord.

To effectively play the D7 chord, the first thing you will have to do is to make sure your first fingers are placed on the C, G, and E strings, located on the 2nd fret, using them to barre the strings. The next finger is used to play the A string, located on the 3rd fret. When learning this chord, understand that it is a gradual process. Hence, don't get too upset if it isn't perfect the first few times you try it. It can take a while.

Another alternative way of learning the D7 chord will be using a finger to play the G string that is located on the 2nd fret. Ensure that the second finger is also placed in the same location. It should be used to play the E string. If this is done correctly, the A and C strings will be left untouched.

G7 Chord

The first thing that you will notice while playing the G7 chord is that it is a simpler version of playing the D7 chord. The G7 chord can be played in a fairly straightforward process. Make sure that the 1st finger is placed on the E string. You should find the E string on the 1st fret. The 2nd finger should be on the C string. This string can be found on the 2nd fret. The 3rd finger should be placed on the A string. This string can be found on the 2nd string.

Have you gotten all the strings correctly? If you have, then playing the ukulele chord G7 should be seamless.

E7 Chord

The E7 chord is also the 7th chord and is similar to the last two chords, which we have talked about. To play the E7 chord, your hands will need to be placed on the G string. This string can be located on the 1st fret. The next finger will be placed on the C string. This can be located on the 2nd fret. Finally, the last finger will have to be placed on the A string. This string can be located on the 2nd string.

Are you looking for valuable tricks that will help you learn these chords faster? One tip will be making sure that these chords are played using your fingertips. If the E string is proving to be a bit of a challenge, you can try arching your fingers. Doing so will ensure that the E string is muted.

Another way in which you can make the learning process easier for you is to note similarities between chords. For example, the F and A chords are pretty similar. Hence, you will find learning one easier after learning the other. Also, moving between both chords will be more stress-free.

Other Minor Chords

Apart from the major chords that are being used on the ukulele. There are also other minor chords. These will include the A, D, and E minor.

A Minor

The A minor is yet another chord that can be used to play the ukulele. So how can this be played? The best way to play an A minor is by making sure that the 2nd fret, which is attached to the 4th string, is held down. After you have achieved this, try to strum all strings. Usually, the number of string present will be four.

So how can you play the A minor? The first thing you have to know is that playing the A minor is easy. It is, after all, a simple chord. Another reason is that it only needs just one finger to be successfully played. Keeping your hands just right is crucial to executing this chord perfectly.

D Minor

There is also called a D minor. If you are thinking about learning more about the D minor, you will be relieved to know that it actually is quite similar to how the F minor. How can you fret the D minor chord?

The first thing you will need to do is to make sure that your hand is placed on the E-string. Usually, it is recommended that you use your index fingers to make sure that this is achieved. Once this has been done, the next thing will be to place your hands on the second fret. Then make sure that your hands are also on the G-string fretting it. The fretting process is usually done with the middle finger.

The last step will be making sure that the E-string is also touched. The E-string will be found on the second fret. You can accomplish this by making use of the ring fingers. Using the right fingers to fret will make the work easier.

E Minor Chord

The E minor is also called the "Em" chord. To play the E minor, your hands will have to be placed higher up the fretboard. The first thing you will have to do is to make sure that your hands (index finger) are on the second fret. The string will be A-string.

The next thing to do is to make sure your middle fingers move over to an area where E-string is located. Try to fret it in the 3rd fret. After doing this, use your fingers (preferably the ring finger to fret the fourth fret. This will be done by playing the C-string. The diagram below will probably help you understand this better.

While playing this chord, you will probably notice that this chord is one tricky chord to learn. The reason for this is that your fingers will keep sliding across the other strings which are present. To solve this problem, it is important to make sure all strings are touched individually. You will know when this is happening. The absence of buzzing will tell you when you have achieved this.

The most important thing here is practice. This is because, if we practice often, our fingers will get used to the different positions in all the chords we have outlined here.

For the next chapter, we will discuss extensively on the various songs that can be played with the important chords discussed above on the ukulele. It is one thing to know how to play; it is another thing for you to know how to play certain songs that will gladden your listener's heart.

How to Read the Ukulele's Music Notation

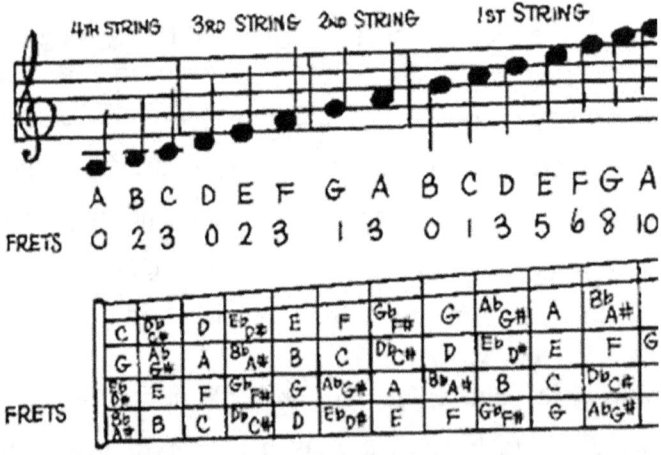

Now, don't get me wrong. You do not need to learn how to read the ukulele's music notation to know how to play your ukulele. While this is true, it is also important you learn it. In the long run, it helps you to understand how the ukulele works better. So having said this, here are the most things to know about reading music on your ukulele.

Musical Staff

There is no better place to start than the musical staff. This is where everything happens. It is often called the foundation and is the area where other notation stays. What is described as the musical staff is horizontal lines? They are usually five of those lines. These lines can be found on every page.

Clef

Of course, the next thing you should know about the clef. The clef always appears at the beginning of the musical staff. It is important to note that not all clefs are the same. There are variants of the clef, such as the bass and treble. Sometimes, more than one clef can be used at once. When this happens, the clef is usually known as the grand clef.

When it comes to the ukulele, the clef, which is usually used, is the treble clef. One reason why this clef fits perfectly is the fact that the uke has a very high range. With this clef, the need to have extra staff will all but eliminated. Are you wondering how you can identify the treble clef? The treble clef can be spotted by its curl. This curl will usually end around the G note. This helps you to understand the entire notation.

Key Signature

The key signature can be found to the left of the clef. What does the key signature do? It helps to identify the notes that are have altered to match with the key. Key signatures are divided into twelve. These 12 signatures contain different types of signs such as the sharp and flat signs. We will know about those later on. If you feel that key signature is absent in the musical staff, you will usually find the key in a C major. These chords will usually come with no signs to show.

Time Signature

Further right comes the time signature. What is the function of the time signature? The time signature is responsible for identifying the counts of the song and how the notes being played all fit. When the time signature is used, there are usually two things that come to mind. These are;

- The number of beats that can be found in a measure
- The particular number of note counts that will signal a single beat.

Many people often find out that 4/4 is the easiest time signature to use. This "4/4" means that the upper number is four beats (using the measure), and the lower is also four, meaning that it is most appropriate to use in counting.

Other time signatures are used such as 2/3 and 6/8

When using 4/4 as the time signature, many people have the alphabet C to signify common time. It might prove very useful in the future.

Notes

The notes can be found on the musical staff. You will usually see them as dots on the staff. However, the notes could also be represented as a space or a line. It is important to note that sometimes, the lines of the staff may actually run out of space. When this happens, additional lines can be added. These lines are often referred to as the ledger lines.

Notes on lines, as earlier explained, will often start with the middle C. This can be found on a ledger line, which will often be lower than the staff. The others will be "E," "G," "B," "D," and "F."

If the notes happen to be in spaces, then it will most likely start from D. This can be found in the middle of the ledger line and the rest of the musical staff.

Accidentals

The next thing we will discuss is the accidentals. The accidentals are made up of the sharps, naturals, and the flats. The C major scale is a good example of natural signs. The sharp sign will often be described as a pound sign. "#" is how it looks like. When it is used, this means that the note will have to be raised ½ step (a single fret).

A flat sign is fundamentally different. It is often described as a b in its lower case that has been altered. When it is used on notes, it signifies that the note will have to be lowered ½ which also means by a single fret.

The natural sign, on the other hand, serves more like a reversal. It ensures that any note that has changed is reversed to its original state.

The key signature, as earlier discussed, makes understanding the accidentals easier. The key signature can be described as a compressed back of accidentals, which signals the notes that have been modified and when. All you have to do is to make sure that you apply them appropriately.

Repeats and Measures Signs

When dealing with music, you will quickly realize that each piece of it is broken down into measures. Measures are often described as vertical lines. These lines will often cut across the entire musical staff.

The measures come with just the right number of beats that the time signature shows on the piece of music. The repeat sign will often function the same way as a measure and is often described as a thick vertical line or a small vertical line, or even dots. These dots can be found in the middle line.

Repeat signs, therefore, can be right-faced or left-faced. When you see a repeat sign which is right-faced, then you really don't need to focus on that. However, when confronted with a left-facing repeat sign, then you will have to either start all over from the beginning or go back to where you last saw a right-facing sign.

Duration of Note

Note durations will help you to fill up your measures. The truth is that a piece of music should immediately tell you some things about its note. These things include the particular pitch, which will be preferable, and the duration that it will take to play this pitch. This is what is referred to as note duration. The duration of the note will depend on the type of note that is used.

For example, using a whole note will mean playing the pitch for the longest period. Sometimes, it can take up to 4 counts. A whole note is often described as a dot that is shallow and does not have a stem. The half note comes next and can often be completed in just two counts. The quarter notes take about four counts to play, and the 8th note will take about eight counts to play. There are so many others.

The time duration is often calculated using the 4/4 time signature.

Ties

This refers to any line (curved) that serves as a link between two notes. The two notes that are linked together will also be linked to the location of the pitch. However, if they happen to be of different pitch, then they will be known as a "slur."

It is important to note that ties tend to spread notes into various measures. It is also possible to take more than two notes and tie them together. These will then form double stops and chords. This will, in turn, lead to durations that are longer.

Rests

This follows the idea in the note durations. The only difference is that rests are not pronounced. It is completely silent. The rest equals a note. In other words, when rest is said to be quarter, it will last as long as a quarter note. However, silent, it will be.

Dynamics

Dynamics will refer to the particular volume that is suitable for that particular set of notes. Most signs belonging to this concept are gotten off words with Italian origins. These words will include piano and mezzo, among others conveying meanings of soft and moderate, respectively.

Piano will usually be portrayed as "p," mezzo as "m," and forte as "f." It is important to note that these dynamics can be repeated in a certain way to convey the right meaning.

Other Things Worth Noting

Hopefully, you have learned most of the basics about the ukulele and how to read its notations. Here are some other things worth knowing;

The Fermata Sign

This sign is often known as the bird's eye. This gives you the ability to hold up the notes. This holds even after the note duration has passed. This sign is often identified as an uncompleted circle. This circle will have a dot right in its middle. A fermata will come upside down and faced up. The position of the fermata is dependent on the note stem.

Accents

This allows you to use a much higher volume on the notes. The accent's sign is divided into two. These are the normal accents and heavy ones. A normal accent can allow you to lift the volume higher than usual. A heavy accent will double the effect. You are more likely to find the heavy accent to your right and the normal ones to your left.

Staccato

Their dot will usually identify these notes. This dot is usually located just below the notes. Sometimes, it can appear above, depending on the position of the stem. This note indicates that the note should be stopped almost immediately after it starts. In fact, the meaning of the word is "detached."

These are the basics you have to know, and hopefully, it makes enough sense to push forward. To learn how to read music, you will need all the arsenal you can carry. This is what we will discuss next.

Tips and Tricks to Reading Music

When it comes to the ukulele, many skills can help you master the art of playing the instrument. Without a doubt, one of them will surely be the ability to be able to read music and chords effectively. While this might sound pretty straightforward, it usually poses a big problem for people who want to learn more about ukulele and music in general. Do you feel this same way? If you do, do not fret. We have got you covered.

In this chapter, we will be looking closely at music and chords and the various tricks and tips for reading music and chords. By the end, you should have enough knowledge to make real progress. Let's jump right in then.

Understanding How to Read Music

Music is an amazing thing. However, reading music is quite a different ball game. For most people who have a limited understanding of how to play the ukulele, they spent a lot of time trying to hear the songs rather than read them. While this might have worked in some circumstances, the effect is usually limited. Just hearing the song and not actually reading the song will usually lead to a limited number of songs that can be played.

Another reason why people do not read music is simply down to fear. Just looking at a piece of music can inflict a large dose of fear. However, the good news is that reading music is actually possible. Ready to find out more? Let's look at some preliminary steps which are sure to help you grasp the tips. Afterward, we'll go a tad deeper. Here they are;

Be Ready Mentally

There is so much that can be won or lost mentally. This is one of them. Before you actually start to learn how to read music or learn any chords, the first thing you will have to do is to be ready. How can you achieve this? The first thing is to make sure that you erase every knowledge which you thought you had about songs and ukulele. This is especially important since you probably are just starting out.

Also, make sure that you remove the traces of fear which you will probably feel. Try to remind yourself that you are surely not the first person to learn about the ukulele or about reading music. Once you have your mind cleared and you feel mentally ready, then you should take the next step.

Method Book

Now, the next step will be to get yourself a good method book. Are you wondering what a method book is? Method books are usually used to teach the various ideologies that come with reading music. When starting, you should probably start with a method book that introduces new concepts. Where can you get a method book? Well, that's quite easy. Method books can be gotten from local music shops all around you and are quite affordable.

Method books help to reduce the complexity of reading music over time. It does this by taking you through the journey gradually and in a logical sequence. Once you have gotten your method book, then it's time to get to the next step.

Get a Mentor

Now, getting a mentor is not in any way compulsory. However, there are a lot of benefits that are attached to it. One of such benefit will be helping you with some new concepts. The truth is that most of the things you will be learning about reading music for the ukulele will be introductory matters at first. However, they can still be quite tricky, to say the least.

Getting a mentor will offer you some relief and help. You will be able to understand some important aspects of reading music and be able to monitor all other aspects of the learning process.

Practice Everyday

Another preliminary thing to keep in mind will be the need to practice every day. Believe me, you have no idea just how important it is. The trick to learning how to read music is to make sure that you get as familiar as possible with the music and its patterns. Doing so will ensure that the learning process becomes a walkover.

Therefore, make it a goal of yours to practice everything. You surely cannot go wrong.

Master the Act of Sight-Reading

Now, this is a very important concept. This simply refers to the ability to read the music right from the sheet at a very high tempo. This also means that the option to hear what the material has to say before reading is out of the option. It is an incredible skill, to say the least.

This is one skill which you have to master. The fastest and most reliable way to master it is by practicing with the pile of music which has been made available to you.

Here are some of the preliminary things you have to know before you can effectively learn how to read music and chords. Now, let us see some of the tips and tricks which will allow you to read music more effectively;

Understand the Power of Rhythms

One of the most important things to look out for when learning how to read music will be your rhythms. Understanding how rhythms work will give you a good idea of how the entire music sheet is going to play out. Rhythms vary and are quite a lot. For you to become really good at sight-reading and reading music, then you have to be really good at learning your rhythms.

Examples of rhythms will include 4/4, 6/8, and so much more.

Chords and Songs on the Ukulele

There are a lot of songs that you can easily play on the ukulele. Playing songs on this instrument is as simple as playing it on the Guitar on any other musical instrument that you may find yourself with. In the ukulele, once you have learned how to play with the different chords in the previous section, you will be able to play any song you want with ease.

There are a lot of tricks you have to take note of when you are learning how to play the ukulele. In this section, we will be going through these tricks so you will be able to learn them and master them to the fullest capacity. Note that the next sections are not to identify the kind of songs that can be played. We will discuss that in the next chapter. The next parts of this section are the best tips you will have to take to ensure mastery.

- Start slowly and start from the basics. This is one of the most important things you need to learn when you are dealing with chords and songs. Once you have a firm grasp of all the basic chords you need to start with, you need to start playing slowly, and from there, you build yourself gradually. In the beginning, you need to start with easy songs that have little or no chord changes while you are playing. Along the process, you will be able to speed up your play if you practice constantly.

- The first tip we will give you in this section as a guide to learning the ukulele is to determine the key. Whatever the song is that you want to play, ensure that you know how to start with the right key. Before you begin to play any song, play the audio version of that song on any song audio device. While you are doing this, try as much as possible to listen and grab the key use to play that song. It may be very difficult to get this key, but when you get it, you will go how to start your play.

- The next step to properly learn how to play this instrument is to find the melody. This is a very great tip. Finding the melody is very important. Pick the melody, go slow, and while you are playing, sing along with the music in your head. This will enable you to go with the low of the music and play better.

- It is important to note that while you are learning how to play, it is one thing to know the chords to play, it is another thing to know where the changes will occur while playing. While playing, ensure that you know when the chords will occur. It is not all the songs that the chords will change, but it is important to know when it will.

- While you are playing, you must learn how to listen to the bass. With any song you are trying to play, there is a very high chance that the chord will change during the play. As a player, these chord changes need to be properly monitored to ensure that you do you lose balance during play.

- While you are listening to the songs you intend to play, you need to focus on the patterns guiding the songs and its overall play. In your head, you need to isolate all the instruments and listen to them individually to recognize and flow with the patterns of the song. This is one of the important things you need to know to be a better ukulele player.

- In the songs, there will always be a lot of hard beats that you will come across. As you are learning how to play, you need to learn how to watch the hard beats that you may come across if they are anyone. Most songs that you decide to play often do not have these hard notes, but when they do have them, you should learn how to handle them. This is very important.

- To learn how to play the ukulele quickly and as easily as possible, you need to be around or watch other ukulele players. As a learner, joining a band will improve your overall play greatly because it will give you the morale to be better at what you are doing. While you are watching them, watch their tempo, their lyrics, and their overall play. If you do this consistently, you will see that you will be able to achieve mastery within a very short time. Being around better people is one of the best ways of being a master at any instrument that you may find yourself playing, most especially the ukulele.

- Play and record yourself. It is one thing to play; it is another thing to listen to yourself while you are playing. While you are on the ukulele, you can record yourself and listen to your music while after your play. This helps you in a lot of ways. One of the ways is that you will know the kind of errors that you are making, and you will make a conscious effort always to be better. Once you are listening to yourself while playing, you will notice the ups and downs of the chords you are using to play, and if there are any mistakes, you will correct yourself and try to be better in the next round of play. Recording and listening to yourself is one of the fastest ways to learn this instrument

- Exercise your fingers regularly. Finger exercises are very important when it comes to playing the ukulele. All you need to do is to look for any finger exercise and constantly practice it. It will make your fingers stronger, and you will not get tired of playing easily.

There are several times when you will always feel like giving up. It is a very normal process. What you need to do is to be consistent. Always keep on practicing with different songs until you get it right. The whole process is a long one, and when you need to go through this journey of mastery.

Conclusion

We have learned a lot, haven't we?

It is important to note that among all these chords that I have mentioned and others that I haven't, the most important one is the C chord. As you are trying to learn this instrument, you need to master the C chord before you proceed to learn the rest of them. This is because most of the other chords just have different notes that are a step up or a step down different from the notes on the c chord. The c chord is a major steppingstone when it comes to the mastery of the ukulele instrument.

The next chord you should dedicate more time to learn is the G chord. Playing the G chord is very similar to playing the C chord because most of the notes are the same. For most players, the G chord helps them to play certain songs in a variety of ways that will make sense to the listeners. Once you learn how to play the C chord and the G chord, you will learn how to play other important chords.

The next chord we need to learn about here is the F chord. The different positions used to play this chord have been outlined in the preceding sections of this chapter. The F chord is also an important chord when it comes to playing the ukulele. A lot of ukulele players use this chord to produce melodious songs for listeners. Even while playing for a group of people in a large audience, the use of the F chord in the ukulele helps your play to stand out during the play.

In the next chapter, we will dwell on how you can use the ukulele to play various songs loved by a lot of people. There are a lot of songs that can be played with the ukulele that a lot of people do not know about..

Chapter Five

The Top Songs You Can Sing with the Ukulele

Now, this is getting very interesting.

We have learned about the history of the ukulele and how it has brought joy to the world. We have also learned about the parts of the ukulele. But what use will it be to us if we do not know how to play our favorite songs on it?

Here we go.

First, as beginners learning ukulele chords, we should be aware of things that could occur, especially if it is your first time using the instrument. We have the major chord, minor chord, and the seventh chord, as we have learned in the previous chapter. However, prepare yourself, as difficult chord diagrams may tend to pain your fingers while strumming, especially at the early stage. But you will get used to it with time.

There are over dozens of chords, and we can play them in a hundred ways through the chord chart.

The Chord Chart

While we have discussed chord in detail in previous chapters, the importance of these chords cannot be overemphasized. Learning them is one way in which you can unlock your potential with the ukulele. So let us do a brief recap, shall we?

The major chord starts with the seven major chords; they can be transcribed as A B C D E F G (La Ti Do Re Mi Fa Sol). They are the most important keys to the list. Chord E is difficult, but it is used in most songs. The major chord has a lively tempo and generally makes the player happy.

Then we have the minor chord. This chord is frequently used because it gives songs this wonderful and intimate feeling. The sound it produces helps the player to invest in what he/she is doing emotionally.

A lot of players often underestimate the seventh chord. As a beginner, you will soon come to appreciate this chord as it adds a certain groove and funky feeling to your songs. This chord is often used in uptown and jazz songs.

Moving on.

The beautiful thing about playing the ukulele is that you do not need to know how to read music. You only need to understand chord charts. A chord chart is simply a diagram that helps you to know the exact place to put your fingers when playing a particular chord. It represents the five frets as if you stood up and looked straight at the ukulele.

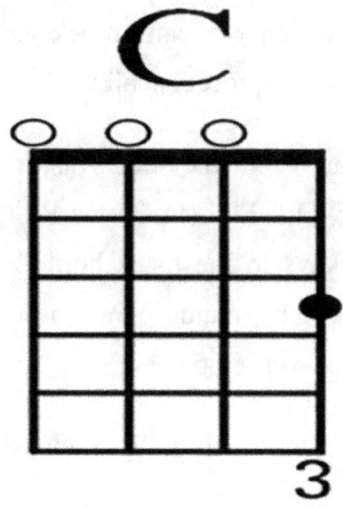

In the chord diagram, we have different parts:

a) Thick horizontal lines: These lines are at the top (as you see in the diagram above), and they represent the nut. However, you need to know that not all chord diagrams start at the nut. If you encounter a chord diagram that doesn't start with a thick black line at the top, a number usually appears at the top right (or left), so you have to use that top line as the fret instead of the nut.

b) Thin horizontal lines: These are the frets. The first thin line is the first fret (below the nut), and the last line is the bottom fret.

c) Vertical lines: These represent the strings. The first vertical line is the G string, while the last is the A string.

d) The dots: Since the chord diagram helps with finger placing, the dot shows you exactly where to place your fingers. For instance, if a dot is on the far-left line between the first and second lines, your hand should be on the G string of the second fret. Easy, right?

e) The bottom numbers: They tell you the finger to use when fretting a certain string.

   1 = Index finger

   2 = Middle finger

   3 = Ring finger

   4 = Little finger

- The top 0s: These are strings that are played open, so you do not have to fret them at all.

All these might look like a lot, but you will understand it with time.

The question now is, how can you use all this information to play a song?

a) Imagine the neck of your ukulele as a glass: One of the best ways of understanding a chord chart is by imagining that the neck of the ukulele is like a glass, and you can see your fingers and fret through it. That way, a standard chord diagram will feel like you holding the ukulele in front of you while holding the fretboard away from you. It becomes easy to mimic everything on the chord diagram on your ukulele that way

b) Mirror image: This is another way of interpreting these charts. Look at the chord diagrams as though you were looking at a mirror.

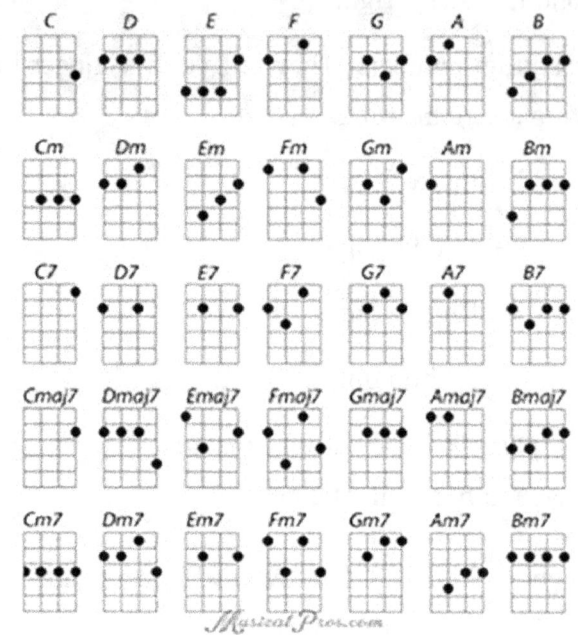

This is an example of a chord chart. C, D, and the like stand for major chords. Cm, Dm, and the like stand for minor chords. While C7, D7, and the like stand for seventh chords.

Top Chords every Beginner must Learn!
Once you learn these chords, the sky is your starting point:

a) **The C Major**: You can play this by simply placing your hand on the first string of the third fret and strumming all four strings. This is often played with the ring (third) finger. Note that your ukulele must be tuned according to the standard – G C E A

b) **The G Major:** the chord diagram for this looks like the chord diagram for D major chord on a guitar. Put your index finger on the second fret of the third string, your ring finger on the third fret of the second string, your middle finger on the second fret of the first string, and then strum all together.

c) **A minor**: Place your hand on the second fret of the fourth string and strum all four strings. You're good to go.

d) **E minor**: Hold down the second fret of the first string with your index finger, the third fret of the second string with your middle finger, and the fourth fret of the third string with your ring finger. Strum them all.

e) **F major:** Put your second finger on the second fret of the fourth string, your index finger on the first fret of the second string and strum all four strings. The beautiful thing about this chord is that it is much easier to play it on the ukulele than on a guitar.

f) **A major**: hold down the second fret of the fourth string with your middle finger and the first fret of the third string with your first finger. Strum all four strings and you are good to go!

g) **D minor:** If you are conversant with the guitar, you will realize that the chord shape of D minor on the ukulele is almost the same as the chord shape of A minor on the guitar. Hold down the second fret of the fourth string with your middle finger, the second fret of the third string with your middle finger, and the first fret of the second string with your index finger. Then strum all strings. Take note that switching between the second and third fingers in this chord is quite common.

So, what if you have practiced hard to play your song, and your ukulele goes out of tune?

Tips Before you Learn to Play a Song

Know the Song Structure

Every song has an arrangement. This includes how the songs are being ordered, the number of verses, the pre-choruses, choruses, and tag end. Write down the lyrics to see the arrangement (make sure you label each section). You should get every meaning of every phrase and word in the lyrics. This shows the details that need to be learned quickly. Use the internet if you have to.

Use the Best Key

As a singer, you have many keys that are used to sing a variety of songs. Melody in songs has low notes and high notes. So, make sure you are singing the melody on the lowest and highest note comfortably. Pick the right key to be able to sing the whole melody range comfortably. If you are learning a song with notes, write down the keys of the song close to the name on the list. As you practice, you will be able to remember faster (having the keys beside the name). If you choose the wrong key, don't give up. Try again and again.

Learn the Melody

At first, learning the contents in its entirety shouldn't be a priority. If you are working on someone else's song, ensure that you sing along with the other singer or vocalist. Keep in mind that you can also read the music sheet and practice it.

With this, you have singled out the melody to get familiar with it. There is a wonderful result achieved when you rehearse the melody differently from the lyrics. Our brains can bring back quickly music and lyrics from separate parts of the brain.

Learn the Lyrics

The best way to understand lyrics is by knowing what the song is all about. Knowing the lyrics and understanding their meaning go together. Put down the lyrics, search for words you don't know in the dictionary. If not conversant with the lyrics, you won't be able to deliver a convincing message to the audience.

Get your own interpretation of what you are saying to them, which helps you remember the arrangement of lyrics verse to verse. Help yourself by memorizing the first verse and sing it out yourself; you can move to the second verse if you are a bit conversant with the first one.

Do the same to the other verses. Sometimes, when you memorize the first line, the rest tend to very easy to grab, make use of emotions like excitement, happiness, anger, sadness, sorrows, etc. and attach them to every word and verse of the song.

Picture a Story

Picture a short movie in your mind that connects to the lyrics and keep playing the movie when learning the song. Our mind loves images and can better recall lyrics that are connected to visualization. Even if the lyrics are very complicated, try to create a storyline from every verse.

Just choose something that you can easily recall, and that can help you remember the lyrics, connect them with something specific like location, things, food, event, etc. It is important to know that our brain is associated with things that are defined. Having such images in our heads will help you recall them easily and naturally.

Mutter the Lyrics with your Mouth

Try singing loud on your own as if you are singing with someone. Do this without an instrument. Loud singing helps you than just memorizing the song. You can also download the memorization tool app; there many designed to help you out. Remember, when you use a different method to advance your learning skills, your memory becomes stronger. Write down the lyrics yourself repeatedly.

Settle Any Range or Pitch Challenge

For example, if you have chosen the right key for the song and in the course of singing the song, you find difficulty in pitching or straining. This could be a result of mismanaging vowels or constant of the words you are singing. Consonance sometimes causes muscle tension in the tongue, which, in turn, affects your voice. Single out the vowel sound for notes and words giving you issues.

Sing Yourself to Sleep

Sing the lyrics again and again before going to bed at night. Research has shown that working on anything before going to bed strengthens our memory. When we wake in the morning, the last thing we thought of before falling asleep comes back naturally because our brain processes things as we sleep.

While doing this, our minds absorb it subconsciously. We are allowing our minds to work on the song while we sleep. You recall it in the morning, sing it before getting out of bed, this is the easiest way of having things get to your long-term memory.

Our brain is frequently looking for ways to change musical information into patterns. Very subconscious. Just try to listen to the song everywhere - in the bathroom, car, toilet, etc. However, avoid distractions to the best of your ability. Let people around you know that you need privacy to learn your song. You can put your phone on flight mode or have a headset on while you put your phone away. Do not also be a distraction to others.

Have a List you Created

Put down your ten favorite songs and learn their lyrics. This can be done on your phone. Start by creating a playlist. Then choose the favorite songs which you will want to learn. Play the song to your hearing often. Try singing to a small crowd, or even if it is a single person, just to know if you are doing well. Also, know that if you are to sing and play together, do yourself the favor of learning to play the music first.

However, it is important to note that while your list will help you, try not to get too attached to the songs. Sooner or later, you will have to learn new songs and get better at it. So make sure that you keep one eye open to adding more songs to your list. That is truly the best way forward.

Recollect the Rhyme

Songwriters and poets have used rhyme for decades because of how beautiful it sounds. It also makes it easy to learn the lyrics of a song. Therefore, let's learn to use the help of rhyme to learn our lyrics. Take a look at the lyrics. Most times, you will notice that in 3 out of 4 lines, a pattern of rhymes can be found.

Listen to a Different Version of the Song

Learning song lyrics in different ways gives a fresh way to strengthen our memory. Working on one method to memorize lyrics is good. However, it could weaken your memory while helping you get to know the song better. Listening to a song performed live is different from the recorded version that our brain knows. Remember, there are thousands of popular songs that have been remixed to feature a particular instrument.

Songs You Can Play on the Ukulele

Warm-up and prep- if you have to play. Make sure your ukulele is well-tuned. You can also include a vocal warm-up procedure. It is very crucial to prepare to sing for a lengthy time.

- Somewhere Over the Rainbow/What a Wonderful World, by Israel Kamakawiwo'ole

A very good song to begin with. One reason is because of how he (Israel) used the world of Bob Thiele and Harold Arlen. He put them together to create magic in the song. This song has a lot to teach you about basic strumming patterns and chords. It is also one of the easiest songs to learn. As a beginner, this is one of the best songs to try when learning to play the ukulele.

- Jason Mraz- I am Yours

This song is modern; the song itself is easy and doesn't have a lot of technicalities. It sounds good while playing. The chord progression is very close to modern pop songs, so it is good if you want to practice singing and learn the ukulele.

- Can't Help Falling in Love by Elvis Presley

This is a challenging song. However, it can be played in several ways. You can either decide to play it in a basic chord progression or jazz it up a bit, but the latter comes with experience. It is recommended that you try starting off with chords and simple strumming patterns. When you have mastered the chord progression and know how to keep the rhythm, you can then change the strumming pattern for the one closer to the original piece. Lastly, practicing and singing this song can yield amazing results.

- Trouble by Never Shouts Never

This song is a bit different, but it is nothing you can't handle with practice.

The secret to this is to start slow and basic. In the introduction, play with a single chord four times per bar, which should later grow into a full strumming pattern. Try to perfect the song before forging ahead to sing and play the song. It is important to note that it might take you a bit of time, and some of the lyrics will strain your vocal capability.

- Riptide by Vance Joy

A straightforward song. If you like modern songs, this will definitely be your favorite. Their various parts might also be challenging. Here, the chord and chord progressions are very simple. When it also comes to the strumming pattern being used, you will see it resembling the classical guitar style. The strumming pattern will challenge you to change from chord to chord. If you are a beginner, it is recommended that you learn to play this song one step at a time. Do not rush. You will become a pro in a couple of weeks.

- Hallelujah by Leonard Cohen

Playing this song on the ukulele gives more energy to the song. It gives it a good vibration, which is rare to see in any other instrument. For this reason, we say this is one of the best songs that can be used to boost your skill on the ukulele because it all comes down to rhythm and accentuating certain chords. It begins slow and soft, but as you keep playing it, the intensity picks up slowly. If you have never done this before, you may find out that you are raising intensity in the wrong places, so you might play loud where it should be soft. Being able to regulate this skill comes with time, and it's something you will use a lot as a ukulele player. This is a top song played on the ukulele

- Hey, Soul Sister by Train

This is a very happy song, so it is sure to get your feet moving when you play it on the ukulele. It doesn't require you to learn any special skill, especially when it comes to the strumming pattern. The chords and progressions are very easy. The only place you might encounter challenges is when you want to sing and strum your ukulele at the same time. In an attempt to learn this, you might put a lot of people off while playing because Hey, Soul Sister doesn't sound the same unless you hit those high notes. If singing is also your interest, this song a good for singing and playing. At first, it will be difficult, but if you push harder, your effort will be worth it at the end.

- Blank Space by Taylor Swift

This song has become popular because of Taylor Swift's ability to turn simple chord progressions into amazing, memorable songs that millions of her fans love, and it is a very good one for beginners. Young ukulele players mostly play this song; the level of your skill determines the beauty of the song. Strumming pattern is one of the regions you can play around a little, although many who play this song use a standard strumming pattern.

- Hello by Adele

This is one of the songs that shook the world because of how amazing it was. It didn't take much time, and it found its way into the ukulele; the outcome was impressive. The song is easy to learn, and you can use the straightforward strumming pattern. It is important to note that strum stress is up to you. Some like to play it fast to get a pop feel while others prefer to take it slowly and turn it into a powerful ballad. The fun in the song is your ability to sing it and make sound great.

- Creep by Radiohead

This song is a bit tricky to play because of how the chord progression is with the singing parts. This song helps you blend both singing and playing. If you wish to take the song to another new level, try moving into chords. The difference is insane.

- The Team by Ed Sheeran

This one of the best songs you can play on the ukulele. Half of the chords in ukulele-playing are simple bare chords. You can decide to make it either simple or complicated for yourself. It also gives room for one to improve himself/herself, especially for players who like to spice things up with a few ticks there or here. You can also create a strumming pattern or make use of standard strumming patterns.

- All of Me by John Legend

The last song we would love you to try is also one of the most challenging songs you can learn using the ukulele. However, with a good practice chord progression, you are in for success. Here, vocals are not difficult to get as long as you strike the right notes and keys. Since there is a high note in this song, the chorus might be a little bit difficult.

Other songs you can play

- Tears in Heaven Eric Clapton
- Upside Down by Jack Johnson

- Tonight You Belong to Me by Prudence and Patience
- I Do/Falling for You by Colbie Caillat

Various songs you can sing using the ukulele with C, G, Am, and F chord

- Count On Me by Bruno Mars
- Out of the Woods by Taylor Swift
- Photograph by Ed Sheeran
- Love Story by Taylor Swift
- Fight Song by Rachal
- The Monster by Eminem featuring Rihanna
- Make it Shine by Victoria Justice
- Leave it All to Me by Miranda Cosgrove
- Play my Music by Camp Rock
- Dear Maria, Count Me In By All-Time Low
- Force of Nature by Bea Miller
- Shark in the Water by V. V. Brown
- Fidelity by Regina Spektor
- Will you be so Kind? by Dodie
- Hold me Down by Hasley
- Bad at Love by Halsey
- Back to December Taylor

Key Points to Remember While Practicing

1. It is in our nature to forget most of the things we learn newly. So, ensure you make it a habit to keep practicing. Try not to practice blindly. Keep a record, whether mentally or otherwise, of the songs which you are learning. This, combined with progress in reading music, will help you to make progress.

2. Start regular practice with little breaks; it could be a one hour break. Just make sure you take a break. Not taking a break will eventually wear you down and lead to low productivity. One hour break will do just fine now and in the long run.

3. In the next few days, continue by increasing your gap between practice sessions. Your practice sessions are where you make things happen. However, with time, you should be improving. So slowly cut yourself some slack.

4. Be careful not to memorize in long practice sessions. Make practice short, giving your brain time to process the lyrics. The truth is that once your brain can process what you are learning and keep it stored in your head, then you should be able to move forward.

5. The better quality of sleep and rest we have, the best we get out of memorizing song lyrics. So, make sure that you get some rest. It keeps your mental state alert. So make sure that you go to bed on time every day.

6. Do not learn a piece of music from the beginning to its end and then start memorizing it. It will be a complete waste of time. Try to really understand the lyrics of the music before trying to memorize.

7. Learn songs one at a time. Don't jump from one song to another. You must be done with one before you learn another, no matter how hard it is. Being uncomfortable is the only way you can grow.

8. Start with hard songs. From then on, the extent of your progress is up to you. To make sure that you meet up with your targets, keep a target calendar to track how much you have achieved. However, there is absolutely nothing wrong with deciding to go with simpler songs instead.

Conclusion

In this chapter, you have learned what a chord chart is, and how you can use it to master the ukulele with the speed of light! You have also learned the major chords every beginner must know. Furthermore, tuning should no longer be a challenge for you, as you have learned how to tune your ukulele accordingly.

Remember, practice makes perfect. For everything you have just learned to stick in, you must practice and practice. However, ensure that you do not learn under pressure. If you get frustrated at any time, please take a break and return to it when you feel like playing again. There is no gain in forcing yourself to do something when you are clearly fatigued. In your right state of mind, you will be better focused and determined.

If you have been playing alone, it is recommended that you get a partner or partners. This is one tip that a lot of people underestimate. First of all, learning to play with others teaches you great team-building skills. Secondly, it exposes you to different songs and the various ways other players play them. Remember, one of the benefits of playing the ukulele is to belong to a community where you can share interests and desires. By belonging to a group, it becomes easier to engage with a community or even start your own.

Furthermore, you should also try sharing your gift and knowledge, even though it isn't well-formed. This is one effective way of mastering the art. You do not need a huge class. You can start by talking to your family members, or by creating both music and tutorial videos on various social media platforms. Finally, if you must strive, you must be ready to put in your best at all times. The bigger thing is consistency in practice over time. Never see yourself above making mistakes because fewer mistakes show great improvements.

Chapter Six

Gaining Experience after Seven Days

A re you having any difficulty reading all of the words from this book? Most likely not. Was it always this easy for you? Think back to the time when you were still learning how to read. Try to recall all those times you came across a difficult word. You most likely felt you would never know how to pronounce them all. You surely needed all the help you could get from the people who already knew how to read well. But as the years passed, reading no longer felt like work. You gained experience. You began to understand the principles behind pronouncing words properly. And you probably can now pronounce words you've never even seen before. Reading has most likely become a piece of cake.

You might be wondering what reading has in common with playing the ukulele. Well, they both share something in common. They both need something to improve your skills in them - experience.

So far, you have stuffed your brain with the know-how of playing this stringed instrument. It must be wonderful for you to learn this much so far. However, you must realize that simply having so much knowledge isn't enough. You need the experience to complete your training. And no, you don't have to buy it. It isn't sold anywhere. In fact, the beautiful thing is that only you can produce it eventually.

In the previous chapter, you saw the beautiful songs you could play with your amazing stringed instrument. But you are not going to play them effortlessly just yet. You are going to need a handful of experience to be able to play them well.

You are going to need a lot of experience to harness your newfound skill. It'll guide you from the way you hold the instrument to the way you play.

Now you know about a key factor that will determine how successful you will turn out to be while you continue to play this wonderful stringed instrument. A dream of being one of the best ukulele players might seem farfetched, but it is not impossible.

However, gaining experience is going to require a lot of work. There will be a lot of ups and downs. A lot of times, you will probably get frustrated because you will feel you aren't getting it right. It's also going to require a lot of time. But it's definitely worth it. And here's why:

It gets better- At first, playing the ukulele isn't going to be a walk in the park. Your fingers are not used to playing, so they might get a bit clumsy. You might find it is difficult to sing while playing your ukulele because your brain will have to get used to performing these two tasks at the same time. You might find it hard to strum effectively or play the chords very well.

However, the fact remains that experience makes it get better. Your experience meter gets filled with each time you practice. And someday, you will have little or no difficulty while you sing and play simultaneously. With time, strumming patterns will come naturally to you. Eventually, you will be playing those songs you have always wanted to play.

Injury reduction- Because you are a beginner, you will probably be applying too much pressure with your fingers while fretting and strumming.

This is only natural because of your level of concentration, which will be quite high, causing your muscles to tighten on the strings preventing you from loosening up while you play. And you might not even notice.

The Aftermath? Sore Fingers

However, it's not going to remain like that. As you play more and gain more experience, you will not have to be so tensed while you play anymore. You will be more relaxed while playing. And the best part is that you don't have to deal with so much pain in your fingers any longer!

It is a transferrable skill- It is common knowledge that the ukulele and the guitar have similar features. Due to this fact, learning to play the ukulele will make it easier to learn how to play the guitar. And not just the guitar, you will be able to play other related instruments.

Take note that all stringed instruments do not share exactly the same techniques while playing. However, they have similar motions. In addition, your brain will have gone through the same process of learning rhythm patterns before, so it will not be as stressed as the first time while you learn another instrument because you must have learned all the basics. This is great news if you've always dreamt of playing multiple instruments.

Tips on How to Gain More Experience
There's an old theory proposed by a famous author that indicates that it takes 10,000 hours to get really good at any skill. 10,000 hours! Now that's a lot. Luckily, research shows that it may take you much less time than that. But you're still going to have to devote a lot of time to learning a new skill and learning how to play the ukulele, and play it well, is no different.

Much like learning any other skill, learning to play the ukulele will take you a considerable amount of time and effort, but at the end will prove worth it. This chapter is going to help you see how best to utilize the time you devote to learning to play the ukulele, as well as other important tips on how to maintain your instrument and get the best out of it. It's also possible that you feel you're stuck and don't seem to notice any progress or development in your skill in playing your instrument. This type of frustration is very real, and you may be surprised to know that it happens to more of us than you think. This might be just what you need. It will include information that is vital to everyone within the skill spectrum, ranging from beginners to advanced ukulele players.

So what are some of the ways you can gain more practical experience after the seven days of learning are up? Here are some salient points

Spreading your Horizon

The thing about learning a musical instrument is that the learning really never stops. You will keep on learning a lot of new things as time pass by. This is the same as the ukulele. When the seven days are up, there will be this sense of accomplishment that comes with it. However, if there is any better time to press on, it is now. There is so much more to learn when it comes to the ukulele. So get up and try to broaden your horizon.

Are you wondering how you can achieve this? One way to do this is to try to play new things and songs. You could also take on a new musical genre. You could also try to play your ukulele using a new technique. Just make sure that you never rest in your comfort zone. Keep struggling to make progress. Always make sure that you are learning more and more. By spreading your horizon, you will be bound to make progress and gain experience.

Take Courses

While this book will ensure that you learn everything you need to play like a pro, it never hurts to keep learning. There is so much more to the ukulele than the basics. One way you can learn and gain practical experience is to take courses.

Fortunately, there are many ways in which you can take courses on playing the ukulele. The world has advanced to a stage where these can be easily taken online. However, while taking courses will be great, ensure that these courses are practical. Make sure that they add value to your game. If it doesn't, attending the course will not automatically or magically make you better at playing the ukulele.

Meet other Players

Experience is practical. Time has shown over time that learning from someone better at a skill is one of the best ways to make improvements. Sometimes, you need to talk to other ukulele players who have played for longer periods.

So make out time to socialize and interact. What are some ways in which you can do this? One recommendation that we make is that you check out forums online where most people interested in the ukulele meet and talk. Trust me; the experience will be beyond your wildest expectations.

Teaching

It is a known fact that one of the best ways to solidify what you know is by teaching. Being a teacher is often described as one of the more genuine things to do. So try to teach someone how to play the ukulele. You could start with the basics and go deeper gradually.

Teaching someone what you know will spur you to gain more experience and become more of a professional. There is nothing you will not be able to achieve.

Your Ears are Gold

Your ears are gold when it comes to playing your ukulele. Being a professional means you have to learn to listen more with your ears and less with your eyes. How can this be achieved? One way to do this is to get yourself an app that focuses on improving your ears.

If you can learn to listen more with your ears, your ability to recognize will increase. This, in turn, will lead to more experience in the ukulele field. You will realize soon enough that your ability will be golden too.

Learn from your Mistakes

The only time that you become a loser is pretty much when you give up. So make sure you keep trying no matter what. Try to understand that in the world of the ukulele, you are bound to make mistakes. The important thing remains how you react to those mistakes.

Therefore, you must learn to pick yourself up when those mistakes are made. Pick yourself up and keep practicing. Soon enough, you are bound to get your rewards.

The Ukulele Festival

If you are always fussing about learning how to play like an expert, then you will be excited at the chance of going to the ukulele festival. The ukulele festival holds so much to offer to someone that is just starting out to play. One advantage is that it allows you to see many techniques and styles of play on show. This will allow your creative minds to get things and will help you to put things into action.

Another benefit that attending the ukulele festival will bring is the ability to meet other people interested in the ukulele directly. There is nothing that sticks better than advice that is gotten from direct contact with people.

Learning about the ukulele is possible and can be done in a short period. However, the improvement stage will last for a while. We can't wait to see how it all turns out for you.

Practice Everyday

At the end of the day, attending festivals and taking courses will only get you so far. What will ensure that you move forward with your goal will be more practice? So make sure that you do the same with the ukulele. The more you practice the ukulele, the more it will come naturally to you.

So how can you make your practice more interesting? Try to practice with a target always in your mind. You can do this by setting to set goals for yourself. You could set a target of learning new songs every week or learning a new chord. So make sure you practice every day. You could also take breaks. You cannot achieve much when you are tired. So make sure that you take your learning process to a whole new level.

Dynamics

Remember, we first discussed the dynamics in chapter four of this book. Dynamics is clearly one of the fun things of the ukulele. To progress, you will need to play your dynamics more and more.

Once you can learn the dynamics, you will play the ukulele so much better. Dynamics is just waiting for you to learn it. Don't disappoint.

Conclusion

It could be that this is your first instrument, or maybe you're just looking to add one more to the array of instruments you are skilled with. It could also be that you plan to play the ukulele professionally, or it could be that this is just a hobby for you. Regardless of what side of the aisle you fall on, learning to play the ukulele will be a wonderful experience. The points in this chapter are to make sure you become the best you can be in the most efficient manner and do so as quickly as possible. Let's look at some of them again to help you summarize what you need to do;

- After buying a good ukulele, take good care of it, tune it regularly, and hold it properly.

- Learn the basics first - the basic chords and strumming techniques. After this, you can progress to more complex chords and playing techniques to add variety to your music.

- Take breaks and repeat while playing slowly to build up muscle memory and develop the needed skills.

- Pay attention to your timing and use a metronome to help you stay in check.

- Listen to others' play to learn new techniques and listen to yourself play to improve constantly. This will greatly help with identifying any problems you may have.

- Take care of your hands and fingers. After all, they're the real instruments. Cut your fingernails and do strumming exercises. This will help improve your playing a lot.

- And lastly, have fun with it! Really. It will do way more than you think. Oh, and sing along; it helps.

The ukulele is one of those instruments you really can't enjoy playing. And it is great for kids and adults alike. The internet is your friend on this journey of learning how to play the ukulele. Do you need help learning how to play the chords? Use the internet! Do you want to watch some of the best ukulele players, so you learn from them? Use the internet! How do you find your favorite songs so you can play along? Use the internet! And finally, PRACTICE! This is pretty self-explanatory. The only way you'll get better at playing the ukulele is if you practice properly and regularly. Practice makes perfect, and experience, simply put, comes with time. So take your time; I dare say the journey is the fun of it. Research says you don't need to practice for 10000 hours, but it won't hurt, right?

Conclusion

Ukulele- The Instrument of your Dreams

Everyone that has been touched by the sound the ukulele produces and the joy it brings can testify that this instrument is one of the greatest gifts the world has received. It has stood the test of time by surviving civilizations, environmental changes, and most of all, surviving cultural changes. In this book, you learned about the history of the ukulele, how it came to be, how it survived generations of civilization and cultural changes to be able to survive and emerge. Its popularity and fame have spread across the world, and will continue to spread as more and more people become aware of the benefits of playing this amazing instrument.

At the beginning of the book, a promise was made. That promise was that this is going to be the last book you will ever need to read on the ukulele. With tips and tricks of learning the chords now deeply entrenched, you shouldn't have any difficulty learning the ukulele.

Research has shown that people tend to be committed to something when they know the benefits or the reasons behind it, and it generally applies to everyday life. People always do things when there is a reason behind it or a benefit they are trying to gain, so this book doesn't just teach you how to play a couple of songs on the ukulele, but it also explains the major benefits behind playing it so that your commitment will become stronger. I hope it worked!

You have also learned the musical notation of the ukulele. You have learned concepts such as time signatures and key signatures and how they influence the duration of the song that is being played.

We have learned quite a lot, to say the least, from the modern-day history to the various songs that you can play with the ukulele.

Then we chords and diagrams, which are easy ways for players to read music at all levels. Vertical lines in this type of diagrams represent the strings. For stringed instruments, you must note the tablature. In any musical instrument, the fingerings are very important, so be sure and remember that you must learn to place your fingers appropriately.

So here we are, ladies and gentlemen!

If you have come this far, give yourself a pat on the back for a job well done! Your efforts and consistency will soon be rewarded when you start enjoying this instrument.

It is impossible to deny the joy, love, peace, and harmony that this instrument creates in the lives of people that listen to its sound. This is one of the few instruments that has managed to stand the test of time, regardless of location, environment, event, people, etc. If you are looking for a way to develop and harness your musical skills by learning a musical instrument, the ukulele is a great place to start!

As we have mentioned earlier, there are so many reasons why you should play the ukulele. Learning the ukulele can take time, even after the basics have been learned. However, you can be sure that what you have learned will be rewarding.

Remember when we said that you could learn the ukulele in a short time? Yes! There are several ways you can achieve this. Try to maintain the right posture, tune the ukulele accordingly, hum the lyrics of the song as you play, and sing while you play basic patterns. It will help a lot!

Learning more about the ukulele is a journey. We hope that with our help, you are well on your way. Have fun!

References

John King and Jim Transude 2007. A Strum through 'Ukulele History. (http:www.nalu-music.com/?p=96) Accessed January 17th, 2020.

SANDOR NAGYSZALANCZY, 2015. The Birth of the Ukulele. (https://www.ukulelemag.com/stories/the-birth-of-the-ukulele). Accessed January 17th, 2020.

https://www.ukulelemag.com/stories/your-first-ukulele-lesson-a-beginners-guide-to-playing-ukulele

https://www.ukulelemag.com/stories/your-first-ukulele-lesson-a-beginners-guide-to-playing-ukulele

https://ukulele.io/why-everyone-loves-the-ukulele/

https://littlecornerofamusiclover.com/11-things-i-wish-i-knew-when-i-started-playing-ukulele/

https://www.musikalessons.com/blog/2017/08/playing-ukulele/

https://www.musicianauthority.com/how-to-strum-a-ukulele/

https://ukuleletricks.com/how-to-play-a-c-major-scale-on-ukulele/

https://ukuleletricks.com/how-to-play-an-f-major-scale-on-ukulele/

https://ukuleletricks.com/5-different-ways-to-play-a-c-major-chord-on-ukulele/

https://takelessons.com/blog/basic-ukulele-chords-easy-songs-beginners-z10

https://www.merriammusic.com/school-of-music/easy-ukulele-songs-for-beginners/

https://ukuguides.com/beginner/10-ukulele-tips-for-beginners/

https://www.liveabout.com/basic-ukulele-chords-4686692

https://www.learntouke.co.uk/how-to-play-ukulele-g-chord/

https://ukuleletricks.com/how-to-play-a-c-major-scale-on-ukulele/

www.ingramcontent.com/pod-product-compliance
Lightning Source LLC
Chambersburg PA
CBHW071520080526
44588CB00011B/1497